ONLY FOOLS

★★★ and ★★★

HORSES

THE

~~NEW YORK · PARIS~~ PECKHAM

ARCHIVES

TROTTERS FLAT

Lovely Jubbly!

For John Sullivan

1 3 5 7 9 10 8 6 4 2

BBC Books, an imprint of
Ebury Publishing
20 Vauxhall Bridge Road,
London SW1V 2SA

BBC Books is part of the Penguin Random House
group of companies whose addresses can be found at
global.penguinrandomhouse.com

 Penguin
Random House
UK

This book is published to accompany the television
series entitled Only Fools and Horses first broadcast
on BBC One in 1981.

First published by BBC Books in 2016

www.penguin.co.uk

A CIP catalogue record for this book is available
from the British Library

ISBN 9781849909242

Author: Rod Green
Commissioning Editor: Lorna Russell
Editor: Charlotte Macdonald
Designer: Mike Jones
Supervising editor: Jim Sullivan
Production: Alex Goddard

Printed and bound by Firmengruppe APPL, aprinta
druck, Wemding, Germany

ONLY FOOLS

★ ★ ★ and ★ ★ ★

HORSES

CONTENTS

★ ★ ★ ★ ★ ★ ★ ★ ★ ★

PECKHAM
Borough Council

Department for Waste And Recycling Facilities

MEMO

From: Brian Ashful, New World Estate Supervisor

To: G. R. O'Nimmo, Chief Head Of Waste

Date: 11 March 2016

Dear Gerald

The enclosed stuff was found by one of our operatives at the bottom of the waste disposal chute in Nelson Mandela House. It caught his eye because there were so many official-looking papers. He was not having a shufti for cash, cheques, postal orders or suchlike as that is right out of order and against council rules about scavenging.
His gaffer says he was only checking to see that it all went in the proper recycling bin, and he gave him a hand.

There was nothing of any value in the folder, but it didn't look like something that any sane geezer would have binned, so they decided that it would be best to return it to the owners who might be quite grateful to see it again. I spotted them waiting for the lift, which turned out to be out of order, and took charge of the documents as some of them seemed like council paperwork. It turned out to be much more than just council stuff.

I know you think that I'm just an old bin man waiting for his pension but there's plenty in here that's giving me the heebie jeebies, so I'm passing it all on to you.

Yours sincerely

B Ashful

B Ashful
DWARF

MEMO

PECKHAM
Borough Council
Department for Waste And Recycling Facilities

From: G. R. O'Nimmo, Chief Head of Waste

To: Shaun Taylor, Police Liaison Officer, Peckham

Date: 16 March, 2016

Dear Shaun

Hope you are well. The Christmas do seems a long time ago now, doesn't it? I hear you've been back at work for a few weeks and that you are now off the crutches completely.

I've got to say that, like you, we all had complete faith in the magician being able to whip that tablecloth out from under all those plates and glasses, even with a blindfolded man standing in the middle. Be fair, most of the cutlery stayed in place and a fair few glasses remained unbroken, unlike your leg, arm and collar bone. Looking on the bright side, it could have been so much worse if you hadn't landed on our Lady Mayoress. She did a very good job of cushioning your fall, but who would've thought that such a small woman could vomit quite so much?

Anyway, that'll be the last time we use Trotter Entertainments to book the cabaret. Funnily enough, the Trotter name has cropped up again in the form of this strange dossier. I thought that you might want to take a look. There are a number of documents relating to police matters and some even more serious-looking bits and pieces. I haven't read through all of it. Thought it best to get it to you as quickly as possible.

Do you think that you'll be fit in time for the Golf Society trip to Thanet? We still have a couple of places left and you're bound to have more luck than last year. After all, nobody's buying those Kazakhstani clubs from the market any more, so the chance of you being concussed by the head flying off a nine iron two years running is pretty slim.

Best wishes

[signature]

G. R. O'Nimmo
Chief - HOW

Peckham Borough Council, Police Liaison Organiser's Department

From: Shaun Taylor, Police Liaison Organiser, Peckham [s.taylor@peckham-plod.guv.uk]

To: William W. Williams, Head of Legal Services, Peckham [w.w.williams@peckhambc.guv.uk]

Date: 23 March, 2016

Dear Bill

Thanks once again for all of your help with the various compensation claims following the incident at Christmas. Pity we were unable to prosecute The Great Raymondo but, as you so wittily put it, both he and the other act, 'Tony Angelino – The Singing Dustman', disappeared far more effectively than any of Raymondo's rabbits. I understand the colony has spread throughout the ventilation system in the Town Hall and that plans to exterminate them have met with substantial opposition. Six local primary schools are now involved in painting posters for the 'Save the Town Hall Bunnies' protest march.

I have been through all of the council's employee records and there is no Tony Angelino employed on the bins, or anywhere else for that matter. The DWARF did, however, come up with a folder of very interesting bits and pieces that I have sent over to your office. There is a whole mountain of intelligence in here that we could use on the Trotters, who were behind the Christmas party fiasco, but there are also things in here that could be hugely embarrassing for both the council and our police colleagues, so I simply cannot handle this through my department. It is definitely something for Legal Services. There must be some rules about running dubious enterprises from council property, after all!

Best wishes

Shaun

Shaun Taylor
PLOD

Peckham Borough Council, Office of the Head of Legal Services

From: William W. Williams, Head of Legal Services, Peckham [w.w.williams@peckhambc.guv.uk]

To: Helen Johnson, Housing Allocation Officer, Peckham Council Housing Division [h.johnson@peckhambc.guv.uk]

Date: 31 March, 2016

Hi Helen

Thought it would be a good idea to drop you an email about the package that is on its way to you.

The package contains a number of documents, both private family items and official correspondence with public bodies.

There is a great deal in here that is of interest to my department, but I would need a team of lawyers working round the clock for several centuries to make any sense of it all and to work out the legal ramifications. As you know, we are working flat out at the moment on the 'Budgie On The Balcony' issue. The European Commission, the International Court of Human Rights and the United Nations have now become involved since one council tenant began keeping a caged bird on his balcony and others extended that liberty as far as keeping chickens, pigs, goats and a Falabella pony. You wouldn't believe the mess in the lift on market day.

Some of the dossier winging its way to you is so bizarre that I have the distinct impression that it might be a hoax. Before I started digging into this too far, I wanted you to take a look because it all seems to revolve around a former council flat In Nelson Mandela House.

The flat was, to the best of my knowledge, rented to the family in question by your father when he was doing much the same job that you have now. There may be a query over whether a temporary filing clerk in his department, Joan Trotter, influenced your father in any way when it came to allocating one of the then new and highly desirable flats in Nelson Mandela House (then Sir Walter Raleigh House) to her husband, Reginald Trotter.

If you could look into the housing issue to see if you can shed any light on that side of things, I would be most grateful. There is no rush to get the package back to me. No rush at all. Take as long as you like. Not urgent.

Yours

Bill Willie Williams

W. W. Williams
Head of Legal Services

PECKHAM
Borough Council

Helen Johnson,
Housing Allocation Officer,
Peckham Council Housing Division,
Town Hall
Peckham

April 29 2016

Heather Jones
Head of Department,
Culture, Religion And Public interest
Town Hall
Peckham

Dear Heather

It was SO nice to see you when you dropped by my office the other day to tell me all about the Save The Town Hall Bunnies project. The bunnies themselves were being really rather vigorous behind the air vent grille, weren't they? As you say, they are SO sweet, if a little pungent.

I have now been through the papers that you were admiring on my desk and have come to the conclusion that there is nothing at all in here to concern the housing department. Flat 127 in Nelson Mandela House (then Sir Walter Raleigh House) was rented entirely according to contemporary regulations to a growing young family in 1960 and was subsequently bought by one of the family occupants, Derek Trotter, with a totally legitimate mortgage from a reputable finance broker in Caracas, Venezuela.

While there is no question of anything even the slightest bit suspect about the renting and sale of the flat, there is SO much of interest in the rest of the folder. There are oodles of perfectly adorable nic-nacs in here. Some look like they have been put together as a bit of a jape – SO funny – while others are just utterly, utterly fascinating. Delightfully nostalgic, I should say, but it's SO not my department and SO totally fits with everything that you are doing. That's why I think I should pass it on to you for you to deal with as you see fit.

Do pop in to see me again soon, or perhaps we could go out for a coffee to avoid being disturbed by those NAUGHTY bunnies.

Speak soon.

Best

Helen

H Johnson
Housing Allocation Officer

P.S. Just noticed that we have the same initials – we're both HJs. SO funny!

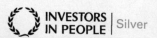

Peckham Borough Council, Culture, Religion And Public interest

From: **Heather Jones, Head of Department** [h.jones@peckham-crap.guv.uk]

To: **Helen Johnson, Housing Allocation Officer** [h.jones@peckham-hao.guv.uk]

Date: 23 March, 2016

Hi Helen

OMG! We really do have the same initials! That's like, really brilliant, isn't it? It must show that we are sort of on the same kind of wavelength, or whatever, right? Because I think that this stuff is simply marverooni. What a treasure trove of totally incredible things.

It just blows your mind when you look at all of this as a complete collection, or if you look at it as lots of little bits, or whatever. However you want to look at it, it is a vastly enlightening, bewilderingly uniquerooni thing. It is like an amazingly honest overview of one ordinary family's experiences as they strive to survive in the harsh world of South East London.

There's only one thing we can do with this precious, faberooni historical document, and that is to share it with the rest of the world. We have to publish it for everyone to see. It's on its way to the printers now.

Must go now as I am meeting a professional rabbit tamer who can help me to gather together all of the Town Hall Bunnies for release into the wild. His name is Del something-or-other. He says he can capture the rabbits by hiding out of sight and making a noise like a lettuce. Totally reasonable fees as well. Amazerooni, huh?

Hugs

Heather

Heather Jones
Head of Department
CRAP

Damien, my boy! If there's one thing that you need to learn in life — and there's actually more than one thing, but I'll teach you the other two later — it's that family matters. Well, maybe not all of 'em, but most families are big enough for you to be a bit choosy, and you have to be a bit careful about the ones you choose.

Pay attention now, because this is all about your heritage, your ancestral megacy. In our family, we carry the Trotter name which, I have to admit, was not always as highly thought of as it is today. Hard work and sound business acumen on my part have put us right up there with your Alex Sugars and Richard Branstons, but previous generations were a right bunch of dipsticks and wasters. Your grandfather, Reg, and his father before him, never did an honest day's work in their lives, but the Trotters weren't always like that.

A geezer I know called Dusty Jack was caretaker at the local library and for a few sovs he would trace your family roots, put together your entire family tree and get it all printed up — just like this. He reckoned that the Trotter name meant that we was, hundreds of years ago, special messengers, trottin' here, trottin' there and trottin' everywhere to deliver very important messages. But we wasn't like postmen. The messages weren't written down in letters because most people couldn't write and, even if they could, chances are that the poor sod they wanted to write to probably couldn't read, so the messengers had to remember the message word for word. The trotters had to be smart enough to understand the message and have brilliant memories to be able to repeat it all. And those are the four things you need to succeed in business — you need to be quick on your feet, you need to have sharp wits, you need to have a photogenic memory and ... something else ... it'll come back to me.

Somewhere along the line our Trotter ancestors lost it all big time, until yours truly came along. And somewhere along the line Dusty Jack lost our ancestors. He was tracing them using birth certificates, marriage certificates, death certificates — and bus tickets and bettin' slips for all I know — but he lost them around the time of your great, great, great grandfather Arthur Trotter. Before him the Trotter family was probably somewhere way up north in the wilds of Yorkshire, and Dusty Jack wasn't too keen on travelling to find out more, even though I did offer to pay his bus fare.

phone Monkey ASAP!
07341152026

PECKHAM LIBRARY

Dustin 'Dusty' Jack
Caretaker + genealogist

101 Peckham, High Street, London

The other side of our family, though, is where we can claim some real class. Your grandmother — my mother — Joan Trotter was Joan Hollins before she married my layabout dad. I always knew she was an absolute princess, and Dusty Jack managed to follow her side of the family back almost two hundred years, where he found a connection to royalty. Your great, great, great, great, great grandmother was, before she married a Hollins, Joanna Royle. We are, therefore, my son, descended from the Royle family. It's no joke — that name makes us aristocats and we can trace our bloodline back as far as King John of England.

THE TROTTER FAMILY TREE

KING JOHN - - - - ADELE DA WARENNE

RICHARD FITZROY - - - - MADELEINE DE PECK

BARON HENRY ROYLE — LADY DAVINA ROYLE

SIR WALTER ROYLE — DAME MARY ROYLE

JAMES ROYLE — MARION ROYLE

ALBERT ROYLE — SUSANNA ROYLE

SAMUEL HOLLINS — JOANNA HOLLINS

JONATHAN HOLLINS — NANCY HOLLINS

KING JOHN!

RODDERS HORSING ABOUT!

TROT INDE!

Happy times!

CAMDEN CHURCH
PECKHAM

WHERE GREAT
GRANDAD JACK
WAS WED TO
GREAT NANA VICTORIA

Camden Church, Peckham

Admittedly, there is a slightly hazy gap of five hundred years or so, but they wasn't so good at keepin' records back then, was they? They didn't have the handroid phones. They didn't have the computers. They didn't have the Filofaxes. All they had was the scrolls — and that's not something they got from one too many pints of mead and a dodgy prawn vindaloo. Scrolls was what they wrote stuff down on back in the day. What the scrolls do tell us is that Peckham was once a huge estate — not the kind like our estate where Nelson Mandela House is — but a country estate where King John came hunting with his knights because the estate had once been owned by his great grandfather King Henry I.

When King John came riding out round these parts he was well away from his missus, the Queen, back in his palace up town, and he liked to put it about a bit, didn't he? To be fair, he was the king, so the birds was all over him like acne. He had more totty buzzin round him than flies around his horse's backside. Well, a man, even a king, can only resist temptation for so long and the King ended up having more flings than one of the little fellas at a dwarf hurlin' contest. The result of one of these croque d'amours was Richard Fitzroy, who became Lord of Chingford. Chingford is, of course, well north of the river, but Dusty Jack says randy Richard was down in his dad's old hunting ground all the time. Most probably every weekend he had off.

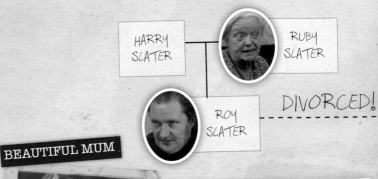

BEAUTIFUL MUM

Damien Xmas '93

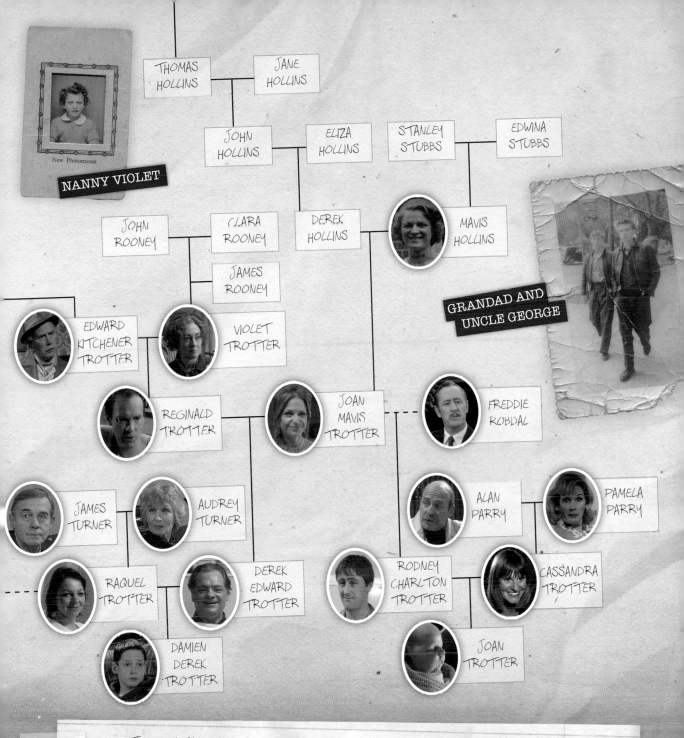

NANNY VIOLET

THOMAS HOLLINS — JANE HOLLINS

JOHN HOLLINS — ELIZA HOLLINS   STANLEY STUBBS — EDWINA STUBBS

JOHN ROONEY — CLARA ROONEY   DEREK HOLLINS — MAVIS HOLLINS

JAMES ROONEY

GRANDAD AND UNCLE GEORGE

EDWARD KITCHENER TROTTER   VIOLET TROTTER

REGINALD TROTTER — JOAN MAVIS TROTTER ----- FREDDIE ROBDAL

JAMES TURNER — AUDREY TURNER   ALAN PARRY — PAMELA PARRY

RAQUEL TROTTER — DEREK EDWARD TROTTER   RODNEY CHARLTON TROTTER — CASSANDRA TROTTER

DAMIEN DEREK TROTTER   JOAN TROTTER

The result of his weekends away was an affair with Madeleine de Peck, who came from our neck of the woods, which ultimately leads us to the Royles. Dusty Jack's investigations — and he never flinched from delving into the records after hours as long as there was a drink waiting for him in the Nag's Head afterwards — show that Madeleine was connected to the Royles, and there we have it — fate a crumply. Okay, so the last of those Royles died around 1300, about five centuries before our Albert Royle, but that's no time at all when you're talking about the length of time that is history, or the length of time your Uncle Rodney used to spend sitting on the bog reading Melody Maker.

DEREK TROTTER
★ ★ ★ ★ ★ ★ ★ ★ ★ ★ ★ ★

CREME DE LA MENTHE
WHAT A CHARMING MAN!

SLATER!

MAD MR MANLY!

Dockside Secondary Modern School
Peckham, London, SE15

School Report _June 1959_

Name: _Derek Edward Trotter_

Form: _Class 9c_

Head Teacher's comments:

I would like to say that Derek is a model pupil. He is never late. He is never badly behaved. He is never ill-mannered. He is never disruptive in class. He is never inattentive. And he is never here. I would like to say that Derek is a model pupil, but I can't because I actually have no idea what kind of a pupil he is — apart from missing. Because he is never in school and has not been seen on the school premises at all this term, I don't believe that I can even recall what he looks like.

Subject Grades:

Subject	Grade
English	A
Arithmetic	A
Mathematics	A
Chemistry	A
Biology	A
Physics	A
Geography	A
History	A
Art	A
Woodwork & Metalwork	A

Watchout! Bendover Benson is about!

Head Teacher's Comments on Grades:

Because Derek has been seen in school less often than The Invisible Man, it has been impossible to award him any grades at all. In this instance, the A's simply stands for Absent.

Summary:

Some might say that the system has failed Derek; that he has slipped through the safety net. On the other hand, Derek, no doubt, feels that he has escaped from a detestable institution. My feeling is that he must now make his own way in the world, where he will either become a burden to society, perhaps even sinking into the murky criminal underworld — or he will rise above it all, using his innate cunning to one day become a millionaire. However, should I ever find evidence to support the allegation recently put to me that Mr Trotter was responsible for loosening all the bolts on my bicycle, causing me to have a rather unpleasant accident going down a hill in Camberwell, no amount of monetary gain will ever make his life worth living.

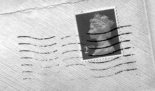

Peckham
Borough Council

Peckham Borough Council
Commercial Licensing Department
Town Hall
Peckham
London SE15
6 September 1986

Derek Edward Trotter
Flat 127
Nelson Mandela House
New World Estate
Peckham
London SE15

Ref: Application for Street Trader's Licence

Dear Mr Trotter

First of all, let me congratulate you on your recent promotion. I note that you are now Chief Executive Officer of TITCO. On your previous application you were still only Managing Director. On the one prior to that you were International Sales Director. Before then you were variously Sales and Marketing Director, Commercial Director and 'Head Honcho.'

I'm afraid I must return your latest application, rejected as so many times before, because some of the details with which you have supplied us appear to be erroneous. Among the many points that caused some concern here was the Company Registration number that you supplied for TITCO, which appears to be identical to the one used by Virgin Atlantic Airways. A colleague here in the Licensing Department has suggested that this may have been some sort of oversight on the part of your New York office as the United States may use an alternative numbering system. Perhaps you also had someone from your Paris office fill out some of the form as not all of it appears to have been completed by someone who could claim English as his first language.

Need I also point out that the photograph you have supplied for identification purposes is wholly inadequate – as are the previous four, also returned herewith? I have had to write to you on previous occasions to advise you that the ID photograph should be of the type suitable for use on a passport. You don't seem to realise that a passport photograph and a holiday photograph are two entirely different things.

Please don't let any of this put you off re-applying for a Trader's Licence, Mr Trotter. Working in the Licensing Department would be exceedingly dull if we thought for a moment that we would never have another of your submissions to look forward to.

Yours sincerely

Daniel Williams
Licensing Office Supervisor

Tel: +44 (0)20   0)2

Peckham Borough Council
Application for Street Trader's Licence

Name: Derek Edward Trotter

Address: Flat 127,
Nelson Mandela House,
Peckham

Physical description (for identification purposes)

Age: Over 25

Hair: Dark, romantic, uncontrollable

Nationality: British, but with strong continental potential

Eyes: One each side of the nose

Ethnic origin: Almost certainly of Royal descent, but without current title

Physique: Imposing yet understated

Height: Just under six feet – better than being just six feet under, though, innit?

Distinguishing features: Charm, wit and taste.

Nature of Business

Goods to be sold: Top merchandise and pukka brand names (eg Goochi, Armany and Cocoa Channel)

Origin of goods: Imported from quality manufacturers around the world and all totally legit.

Price range: Affordable to rock bottom

Projected turnover: Sky's the limit for a modern entrepreneur

Business plan: Buy low and knock the stuff out at a price that makes the punters think they've just got the bargain of the century. No returns, no refunds, sold as seen. 'Caviar empty' as the Romans used to say.

TROTTER'S INDEPENDANT TRADERS

Derek Trotter CEO   Rodney Trotter DIC

Flat 127
Nelson Mandela House
New World Estate
Peckham
London SE15

22 November 1989

Right To Buy Applications
Peckham Borough Council
Town Hall
Peckham
London SE15

Dear Sir or Madamwaselle

As a great admirer of the policies of our exteemed Prime Minister, Margaret Thatcher, it has come to my attention that our glorious leader has decreed that those of us who live in council flats should have the right to buy their flat. Nice one.

I feel that owning my own property would allow me to provide a more stable and homely environment for my dependents, namely my younger brother, Rodney, who relies on me for most things (although he can now dress himself and get his shoes on the right feet most days), and my aged Uncle Albert, who is a war hero and served our country in its darkest hour (and I don't mean them blackouts we had back in the seventies).

If only more of us could own our own homes, we could all take more pride in our surroundings here at Nelson Mandela House. We might even have a whip round so that everyone could bung in a few quid to get the lift fixed.

A home for myself and my family is really all I ask and, let's face it, we've been in this gaff since 1960, so we've paid enough rent over the past 29 years to buy the place at least four times over. Not that money is the major issue here. Buying this place on the cheap and whacking it back on the market to make a hefty profit is the furthest thing from my mind. Providing a home for my family, a place where my brother can flourish and hopefully one day become a productive member of society; a place where my uncle can live out his twilight years in peace and senility – that is all I ask.

Also, I reckon we are due a hefty discount on this place, so we need to talk about a decent price, or maybe you'd like to think about a 'buy-one-get-one-free' sort of deal. Bogofs are all the rage in the commercial world these days, although I don't expect you, as civilian servants, to appreciate the finer points of high finance. I am, however, always available to consult on business advice should you need guidance. You will find my rates extremely reasonable.

Yours sincerely

Del Trotter

Derek Trotter

NEW YORK - PA

AN EXPECTING MUM AND ME IN 1960 AND OUR FIRST TELEPHONE!

Former long-term resident, my daft, but pucker Grandad

My executive parking space!

Peckham
Borough Council

Right To Buy Applications
Peckham Borough Council
Town Hall
Peckham
London SE15
8 January 1989

Mr D Trotter
Flat 127
Nelson Mandela House
New World Estate
Peckham
London SE15

Ref: RTB Appication 147c

Dear Mr Trotter

We acknowledge receipt of your recent letter enquiring about the purchase of the council property at the above address.

You seem to think that, as public servants, we have little or no knowledge of the commercial environment, yet we are used to balancing the books in a number of ways. As such, it is hard to ignore the significant rent arrears you have accumulated.

Clearing the arrears up to date would certainly help us in considering your application to buy. In the meantime, please fill out the attached application form.

Yours sincerely

Henry Johnson

Henry Johnson
Housing Department

Right To Buy Applications **Peckham Borough Council**

Town Hall   Peckham   London SE15

Please answer the following questions as fully as possible.
Use black ink. Illegible, incomplete or adulterated forms will not be forwarded for consideration.

Name: Derek Edward Trotter

Address: Flat 127, Nelson Mandela House, New World Estate, Peckham, London SE15

Is the address you have given the address of the property you wish to purchase?
No, I wish to purchase Buckingham Palace, but this will have to do for starters.

Is the property you wish to purchase your only home?
If I had another gaff, do you really think I'd be living in this dump?

Have you been a council tenant for not less than five years?
We've been in this place for 29 years. Would you Adam an Eve it? You don't get that for murder!

Is the property sheltered housing or adapted for the infirm, elderly or disabled?
Not exactly, but with Rodders moping around like a wet weekend and Uncle Albert living half his life back in the war, you could sometimes think it was a loony bin.

Can you confirm that you have no problems with outstanding debts?
I have no problem with debts. It's them I owe the dosh to that's got the problem.

Can you confirm that you have no outstanding possession orders against you?
I have never been caught in possession of anything that wasn't totally legit.

Do you have a mortgage in place?
Yes. And all completely above board.

Who is your mortgage lender?
Carlos Ramos Esperanza, Finance Broker, Caracas, Venezuela

PECKHAM 2½ᴰ ECHO

Friday 19th September 1958

THE HIGH LIFE IN PECKHAM

Peckham Council tenants will soon have the chance to live the high life in luxury apartments in the clouds.

Report by VINCE PINNER

A new development that would look as much at home in Manhattan as it does in Peckham has been given the green light by local town planners.

Three new skyscrapers are to be built, creating what Mr Herbert Johnson, the council executive in charge of the project, has described as "A city in the sky."

"Each of the tower blocks will house as many tenants as would once have lived in an entire street," said Mr Johnson, "but the new apartments will take them well away from the dust and grime of living at ground level. They will be way up in clean, fresh air. They will have balconies from which they will be able to see to the north as far as Bermondsey. On a good day, to the east, they might catch a glimpse of Canvey Island."

The flats will have all mod cons with up to three bedrooms and toilets indoors. "This is a state-of-the-art housing development," said Mr Johnson. "The three buildings are being constructed using the latest methods, making them quite luxurious and yet cost effective for the council to build."

Built on the site of a former ammunition works, the three buildings are to be called The New World Estate, reflecting how their construction represents a historic step for Peckham. Each of the towers is to be named after a figure associated with the discovery and exploration of the "New World" (America) – Christopher Colombus House, Sir Francis Drake House and Sir Walter Raleigh House.

The New World is not, however, for everyone. "Flats in the new developments will be allocated to those who are in most urgent need of new accommodation," explained Mr Johnson. "Those with growing young families will be given priority."

Construction on the site is due to begin early next year with the three tower blocks expected to be ready to move into by late summer in 1960.

Artist impression

AN EMPTY FLAT...
DUE TO RODNEY'S 'THING'
FOR POLICE WOMEN!

PECKHAM COUNCIL
HIGH-RISE HOUSING PROJECT
THREE-BED APARTMENT LAYOUT, ~~SIR WALTER RALEIGH~~ HOUSE

Nelson Mandela

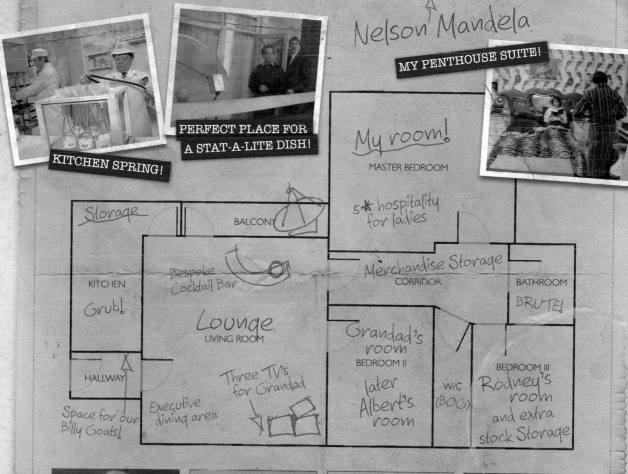

KITCHEN SPRING!

PERFECT PLACE FOR A STAT-A-LITE DISH!

MY PENTHOUSE SUITE!

My room!
MASTER BEDROOM

5★ hospitality for ladies

Storage

BALCONY

Merchandise Storage
CORRIDOR

KITCHEN
Grub!

Bespoke Cocktail Bar

Lounge
LIVING ROOM

Three TV's for Grandad

Grandad's room
BEDROOM II
later Albert's room

W/C (BOG)

BATHROOM
BRUTE!

BEDROOM III
Rodney's room and extra stock Storage

HALLWAY

Space for our Billy Goats!

Executive dining area

MR HERBERT JOHNSON
The council executive in charge of the project which will bring 'luxury apartments in the clouds' to the young families of Peckham.

FUTURISTIC DREAM
Each of the tower blocks will house as many tenants as would once have lived in an entire street.

THE NEW WORLD ESTATE
Each of the towers is named after a figure associated with the discovery and exploration of the "New World" – Christopher Columbus House, Sir Francis Drake House and Sir Walter Raleigh House.

LUXURY IN THE SKY
This is a living room of a typical three-bedroom apartment in Sir Walter Raleigh House. The flats will have all mod cons with up to three bedrooms and toilets indoors.

MILLS QUALITY MOTORS

Melbourne, Sydney, Adelaide, Peckham

G'day Mate

Greetings from down under, Del!

I still can't believe that I couldn't persuade you to join me in Oz. Me — Jumbo Mills, salesman of the century — couldn't sell Del Trotter a dead cert way to make big bikkies.

You would love it here, mate. After a profitable day flogging Rollers, Bentleys and Mercs to people who've got more money than they know what to do with, we could just relax in the sunshine with a cocktail by the pool, kick off our thongs (that's flip-flops to you, mate — I've not gone totally native) and dip our toes in the water. Some days I barely have to do any grafting at all — the order book's as full as a centipede's sock drawer. Still not tempted? Have a look at the enclosed ad that my lovely secretary, Sheila — yes, she really is a Sheila — cooked up.

I do understand about you not wanting to leave your family behind. Shame that drongo Rodney was refused a visa because of his conviction for being caught with a bit of wacky baccy. I bet you were mad as a cut snake when you found that out. He's not a bad lad, though, Del, and you can take the credit for that, bringing him up like you have.

We've come a long way since we were selling eels from a stall outside the Nag's Head, Del, but I will never forget you giving me your last two hundred quid to help me set myself up in Oz. For that, I will always be grateful, and you will always be welcome here either as a business partner or just for a visit. And, of course, if you can bring young Rodders and the rest of the family, there's plenty of room for all at Mills Mansions!

I know that a business supremo like you never even thinks about taking time off, but if you ever do make it here for a holiday, I can do you mate's rates on a bonzer motor!

Yours always

Jumbo

JUMBO IN 1986! LOOKING LIKE A MAN WITH A MIRRORED CEILING!

MEMOREIS OF EELS ON WHEELS

JUMBO AND BOYCIE IN 1960!

...and Jumbo and Boycie (in the Naqs Head) in 1986!

MILLS QUALITY MOTORS

DO YOU DRIVE A CAR THAT'S ABOUT AS EXCITING AS AN EMPTY TINNY?

IS YOUR JOURNEY TO WORK AS DULL AND DRY AS A DEAD DINGOE'S DONGER?

* *

Spice up your life with the dream car you've always promised yourself – a bonzer luxury automobile from Jumbo Mills!

Jaguar Sovereign

BMW M6

Merc 280sl

Rolls Royce

Rolls Royce Silver Spur

Affordable Prices – Affordable Luxury – Affordable Dreams

OUR CUSTOMERS ARE LIKE BOOMERANGS: THEY KEEP COMING BACK!

A NIGHT AT THE OPERA

Love at first sight!
Vicky selling art in the market

FARQUHAR, FARQUHARSON & FARQUHAR

Solicitors & Legal Consultants
Estate Office 2
Covington Estate
Berkshire

Mr Derek Trotter
127 Nelson Mandela House
New World Estate
Peckham
London SE15

28 December 1986

Dear Mr Trotter

We are instructed by our client, The Duke of Maylebury, to inform you that a restraining order has been requested that will prevent you and your brother, Mr Rodney Trottter, from approaching the duke's daughter, Lady Victoria Marsham Hales, himself or any other member of his family closer than a distance of 250 yards.

The incident at the performance of Carmen at the Royal Opera House, where the behaviour of you and your companion, Ms June Snell, was both disturbing and offensive, culminated in Ms Snell vomiting over other members of the audience. This has caused the duke and his family great distress and embarrassment. This incident was, of course, followed by your arrival at Covington House, the duke's Berkshire residence, without invitation, where your behaviour was equally unacceptable.

The Marsham Hales family now wishes to sever any and all ties with the Trotter family. Consequently, you and Mr Rodney Trotter are no longer welcome at Covington House and are banned from the vicinity of the house or from entering any part of the Covington Estate in Berkshire. Should you attempt to enter any part of the estate you will be treated as unlawful trespassers.

We are given to understand that it may not be possible in law to ban you from the whole of Berkshire, as the duke requested, but other members of the duke's extensive network of family and friends are also taking steps to exclude you from their properties, which should effectively restrain you from travelling westwards much beyond Slough.

Yours sincerely

F A Farquhar

F A Farquhar DPhil, LLM, FCILEx

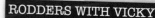

RODDERS WITH VICKY
IN BORING BERKSHIRE

LADY VICTORIA MIXING
WITH ROYALTY!

Gala Performance
of
CARMEN
BY GEORGE BIZET

ROYAL OPE

THE MAN WHO
WAS NEARLY
RODNEY'S
FATHER-IN LAW!

TROTTER, TRIGGER & TROTTER

Business, Financial & Legal Consultants to Trotter Independent Traders
Nelson Mandela House, New World Estate

FURQHAR, FARQURSON & FAQUHAR
Solicitors & Legal Consultants
Estate Office 2
Covington Estate
Berkshire

31 December 1986

Dear Mr Furqurhor

We are in receipt of the letter that you sent to Mr Derek Trotter and wish
to convey his astonishment at your attitude as it is right out of order. He
was under the impression that when The Duke shook hands with him as he
left Covington House we was both singing from the same hymn sheet and
everything was cushty.

Neither Mr Trotter or his brother ever intend to come near your gaff again.
They know where they are not wanted. Mr Rodney Trotter will not be seeing
any sort of posh bint, including snooty Lady Victoria, any time soon either, so
you can stick your restraining order where the sun don't shine.

Furthermore, forthwith and suchlike, you should know that The Duke of
Maylebury and his daughter are no longer welcome around our manor. The
Marsham Haloses should consider themselves banned from Nelson Mandela
House and from entering any part of the New World Estate in Peckham.

Yours sincerely

D E Trotter

D E Trotter DDT, FAB, TIT etc

PARRY

Rodney Charlton Trotter (DIC)
Head of computer section

Parry Printing, Peckham, London

Peckham Rye Grammar School
Peckham, London, SE15

School Report: June 1972

Name: Rodney Charlton Trotter

Form: Class 8b

Attendance and behaviour:

Rodney's attendance record is poor and must be improved. This has been pointed out in letters separate to this report.

Rodney tries hard in class when he can be bothered but seems to find many of the lessons quite frustrating. He has been disciplined this term for persistent non-co-operation in class, claiming, for example, that there was no point in learning about European capital cities as they would all be wiped out when the Russians and Americans instigated 'nuclear agamemnon'. It was pointed out to him that what he meant was 'armagedon' and that Agamemnon was the commander of the Greek army during the Trojan war. At least this shows he picked up something from the lessons on Ancient Greece, although he did at first think that Ancient Greece was what Sid cooked with in the Fatty Thumb café.

Rodney is always keen to join in a discussion in class and will argue his point endlessly, even when he has been comprehensively proved wrong. The suspicion is that this rare enthusiasm is to postpone the resumption of normal lessons.

Achievement:

Rodney shows a clear aptitude in mathematics where he is very quick in using his calculator – so quick, in fact, that it is difficult to catch him using the calculator which is strictly forbidden in most lessons. His mental arithmetic is outstanding, a skill he claims to have learned 'down the market' and 'in the bookies'. He is rather less skilled in English where his essays are peppered with the adjectives 'triffic' and 'cosmic.' Rodney shows some talent in art. He is good when composing abstract works but less so when painting or drawing figures. Like many artists, he struggles with drawing hands successfully, many of his subjects appearing to have only two fingers.

Subject Grades:

Subject	Grade
English	D
Arithmetic	A
Mathematics	B
Chemistry	D
Biology	D
Physics	D
Geography	C
History	C
Art	B
Technical drawing	C

MUMS LITTLE ANGEL
BABY RODNEY

Rodney Trotter
Class 5C

My Peckham - Home of History and Culcha

Peckham is the place where I live. Some people say that it is not a very nice place. I have heard people calling it a dump and sometimes even worse things that I can't put in this essay coz Mickey Pearce got suspended for saying stuff like that to our PE teacher and his dad didn't half give him a wallopin when he got home.

People who slag off Peckham do not know what they are on about. Peckham is right up to date with modern stuff like the flats where we live that are the tallest buildings around. And I should know because I have been right up on the roof pointing a TV hairyal down the river to see if my brother Del could pick up Swedish telly. And if that's not culcha, I don't know what is.

Del is really into all that forin culcha from abroad and so are loads of people who live in Peckham. And when you start readin about the history of this place, you can see why. The first people to live here was the Saxons way back when. They was here even before my grandad was born, and that's sayin somethin. The Saxons was from Germany. Then came the Romans from Italy and some of them are still here. My mate Carlo lives in Desmond Tutu house and his dad is as Italian as a plate of spagetty. He's got an ice cream van that plays the Just One Cornetto song. Well, you don't get any more Italian than that, do you?

Norman

After the Romans, the next people to invade Peckham were the Normans. You might think that they was a bunch of geezers who was all called Norman. Stands to reason, don't it? But there were thousands of Normans and it would be very unlikely that so many blokes should all show up and all have the same name. Mind you, I know at least three people called Colin and there are probably quite a few more out there. If they all turned up in our manor at once it would cause a bit of a stir. Must have been worse when the Normans arrived, though. People would have been running down the street shouting, 'The Normans are coming!' Can't really imagine them all running around shouting 'The Colins are coming!'

The point is though, that they weren't called the Normans because they was all called Norman. They was called the Normans because they came from Normandy, which is in France, although the Normans didn't think that they were actually French, and who can blame them? Anyway, there is an actual place called Normandy, but since there is no place called Colindy, we probably won't be invaded by the Colins. So the Frenchies were here, and in a way they still are because we still use French words in our language, like cafe (caff) and lingerie (nighties) or Asterix (*) and French fries (skinny chips). And of course, loads of people can speak proper French. My brother Del talks the lingo like he was brought up in Paris instead of Peckham.

Being as how the Normans took over the whole country, we had a Norman king, but he wasn't called King Norman, he was King Henry. Old Henry liked to come hunting around Peckham where he owned the whole estate. He wouldn't find much to hunt on our estate, although I did once see a squirrel. Back in them days, though, Peckham was all countryside and they even grew melons and grapes on farms here and there. That was all sold at the local market and you can still buy melons and grapes at the market today on old Nell's stall next to the geezer that flogs three pairs of pants for a quid. 'Three knickers for only a knicker!' is what he shouts.

There is not much countryside around Peckham these days but you can still see a bit of the old river on Peckham Rye. This is important because the whole place is named after the river. The river was called the Peck and the ham doesn't mean bacon, as some people - but not me - might think. Ham is actually an old word for village. So Peckham is the village on the River Peck. The river is all now underground, which is a good and a bad thing. It is a bad thing for fishermen, who can't get at the fish, but it is a good thing for the fish. Not only are they safe from the fishermen, but they are also out of the sunlight, which fish hate because fish don't have eyelids to keep the sun out of their eyes and they can't wear sunglasses because they don't have any ears.

Mind you, it is also a bad thing if you are a duck, totally knackered after a long flight south for the winter and looking forward to cooling your bum in the Peck only to find that it's been covered over. Maybe that's why ducks always look a bit angry.

Today Peckham is a very modern place but history shows us the past and we can see that we have come a long way – a bit like that duck, only through time, not through the air.

Basingstoke College of Art

Application for Enrolment

Surname:
Trotter

First name(s):
Rodney (Charlton)

Previous surname:
Have only ever been a Trotter

Title (e.g. Mr/Mrs/Miss):
Lord

Date of Birth:
2 November 1960

Sex:
Yes please

Nationality:
Bohemian

NI number:
Have never been to Northern Ireland

Home address:
127 Nelson Mandela House,
Peckham, London SE15

How long have you lived at this address?:
Seems like forever

Name of responsible parent or guardian (if under 19):
Del is responsible for most things in my life

How long have you been resident in the UK?:
All of my life apart from one trip to Wales

Will you require accommodation at the college?:
Yes. Two bedrooms, bathroom, kitchen and living room should do it. The cleaner can come on Wednesdays. Colour telly essential.

State your most recent school or college:
Peckham Rye Grammar School for the Artistically Gifted

What courses would you like to study at the college?:
Mainly painting, but not decorating - more your landscapes and what 'ave you

Do you have a medical condition or disability that might affect your studies?:
Sitting for too long in a classroom makes me nod off if I've had a couple of pints the night before and reading for more than 35 minutes at a stretch makes my nose twitch

What are your preferred dates for your first term?:
Mainly blondes who like a good time but no slappers

Please sign and affix passport photo below:
Lord Rodney of Peckham

Watch out Basingstoke, lock up your daughters!

OLD MARKET SQUARE, BASINGSTOKE   PT2974

127 Nelson Mandela House
New World Estate
Peckham
London SE15

Admissions Secretary
Basingstoke College of Art
Peterfield Road
Basingstoke

Dear Sir, Madam or Monsieur,

Re: Rodney Charlton Trotter - Application Mistake

As the legal guardian of my younger brother, Rodney Trotter, I recently received
a note from you rejecting his application to your finely estimuled establishment.

Unfortunately, the application form that you returned as 'REJECTED' was filled in
by a complete plonker as a bit of a lark and was not the form that Rodney should
have sent you. Well, lads will be lads, eh? We've all been there, haven't we?

Rodney may sometimes appear to be a few chips short of a fish supper but he has
always been very handy with his crayons and paints. He painted a very impressive
muriel on the living room wall when he was only three. It took Grandad nearly a
week to scrub it off, although he would have done it quicker if he'd put some graft
in on a regular basis instead of just when the ads was on telly.

The point is that Rodney has set his heart on studying art and it would be a crying
shame if he was to miss out on this life-enhancing opportunity because of a trifling
balls-up.

Enclosed is another one of them forms all filled in proper.

Yours with all sinceritousness

Derek Trotter

RODNEY YOU DIPSTICK!

127 Nelson Mandela House
New World Estate
Peckham
London SE15

Mr Peter Pringle
Principle
Basingstoke College of Art
Peterfield Road
Basingstoke

Dear Mr Pringle

Re: Rodney Charlton Trotter - Expelled from College

I was most shocked and outraged to receive your letter informing me that my younger brother had been expelled from the college and even more shocked and outraged when I learned that it meant he had been booted out. Not furious with your good self, of course, but with a system that can destroy a young life in such a casual manner.

Okay, so Rodney was bang out of order smoking a Moroccan woodbine in the college. It was a daft thing to do and I have never held with people using that stuff. But he only had one puff and it is an art college after all, innit? All artists use a bit of something or other to keep their creative juices flowing. Every fool knows that Vincent Van Coff was off his face half the time. Why else would he cut off his own ear? And old Lenny de Vinchy must have been on something when he painted the roof of the Cistern Chapel. Anyone else would just have given it a quick coat of emulsion.

So how about taking Rodders back? We all deserve a second chance some time, don't we? Turn the other cheek and all that, eh?

yours seriously

Derek Trotter

34

Basingstoke College of Art

Mr Peter Pringle
College Principal
Basingstoke College of Art
Peterfield Road
Basingstoke

Mr Derek Trotter
127 Nelson Mandela House
New World Estate
Peckham
London SE15

Re: Rodney Charlton Trotter - Expulsion Notice

Dear Mr Trotter

Thank you for your letter asking for your younger brother to be reinstated at the college. I am afraid that the college rules are quite clear about these things and behaviour such as that of your brother - which resulted in a criminal conviction - simply cannot be tolerated.

What you refer to as 'a Moroccan woodbine' was in fact a substantial quantity of an illegal substance. One student described it as 'the biggest reefer in all of Spliffdom' which, one assumes, means that even those who have some experience of these things viewed it as excessive.

As you know, the police were called when complaints were received from neighbours about the loud music at the party at which your brother was smoking the marijuana. Statements taken from students present say that the police officer into whose face your brother blew smoke could not effect an arrest because he was 'useless with the giggles' and for the whole of the following day was afflicted with something the students term 'the munchies'.

Fortunately there were other officers present who, with the aid of a bucket of water and a blanket, managed to extinguish your brother's 'joint' and take him into custody. They later said that they would not have believed that such an amount of cannabis was purely for personal consumption had they not actually seen your brother personally consuming it.

The most serious consequence of your brother's actions was, however, on those around him. Students standing in his vicinity were effected quite dramatically. One fell sound asleep standing bolt upright on the sideboard; another began desperately trying to rescue the leprechauns trapped under the carpet and a third has developed an irrational fear of wastepaper baskets.

Because he represents a threat to the smooth running of this establishment and because he has had a dreadful influence on his fellow students, we simply cannot accept your brother back at the college. In fact, he is no longer permitted anywhere on the campus and, if Hampshire Constabulary have their way, he will be banned from Basingstoke completely.

Yours sincerely

Peter Pringle

P Pringle
College Principal

DRIVING LICENCE

UK

1. TROTTER
2. RODNEY CHARLTON
3. 02.11.1960 UNITED KINGDOM
4a. 10.10.1999   4c. DVLA
4b. 09.10.2019
5. TROT 611020RC947 02
7. *Rodney Trotter*
8. 127 Nelson Mandela House Peckham London SE15
9. AM/A/B1/B/f/k/l/n/p/q

74205

ONE OF RODNEY'S EARLY WORKS

a Trotter book

The Brothers

R C ~~Trotter~~ Trotkein

Design and Print, Peckham

Proof cover for
design approval

36

CHAPTER ONE
THE BROTHERS

Two men walked into a bar. Sounds like a joke but it wasn't because nobody was laughing. They were, but then the two men walked in and all of the laughing and chatting and arguing about whose turn it was to wipe the darts scores off the blackboard, just stopped. All eyes, and quite a few heads and noses, turned towards the two men.

The most striking of the two was tall and ruggedly handsome with angular, but not geometric features. He moved with the understated grace of an athlete. He was slim, yet unmistakably powerful. You could imagine the muscles moving in perfect harmony beneath the flowing lines of his exquisitely cut Saville Road suit, although the suit was too cool to show any of that bulgey muscley stuff. He glanced around the bar, his steely blue eyes sweeping the room faster than a Dyson on turbo. A twinkle in those eyes became a faint wrinkle of his nose, then the flicker of a smile on his lips, then a crinkle of his chin before it fell to the floor and scuttled off outside. He looked at his companion and nodded almost imperceptibly towards the bar, which was not itself imperceptible because it took up half the room.

The other man was his brother, but you wouldn't have known it to look at them. They didn't look like they had been brought to us by the same mother. They didn't even look like they'd been brought to us by the same bus. They were so totally different that you would have thought the shorter one worked for the taller one. And that's pretty much the way it was. Blood is thicker than water, so they say, and the shorter one was definitely thicker than his brother.

The short one did not move with the silky smoothness of his taller brother. In fact, he walked like a duck with bunions. He had shifty dark eyes and lots of hair, although a relatively small percentage of that was actually growing out of his head. Mind you there was enough growing out of his nose and ears to knit a syrup for half the Harry Krishnas on Oxford Street.

Conversations around the room sparked up again and the shorter one trolled up to the bar. He was tall enough to reach the counter, but still stood there looking like a Hobbit in a suit by Mothercare.

'Light-and-bitter and a Pina Colada,' he said to the barman in the lisping murmur that he called a voice.

'You're slightly bitter because your penis is what?' said the barman.

The short man's face darkened.

'You heard me,' he growled. He was better at animal noises than human speak. There was no mistaking the anger in his voice.

'Yeah, you heard him,' said the taller one. 'Light-and-bitter and a Pina Colada - fruit, umbrellas, the lot.'

1

THE BROTHERS

The barman took one look at the menace in those steely blue eyes and quickly went about his business preparing the drinks.

'What are we doing in this dump?' said the shorter brother.

'Keep your voice down,' said the taller man.

The short one squatted like a demented gnome and said, 'What are we doing in this dump?'

His brother sighed, stuck his hands in his smaller sibling's armpits and easily lifted him up onto a bar stool, despite the fact that the little one weighed as much as six sacks of spuds, but with less brains.

'We are here to blend in, mix with the locals and find out where the diamonds are,' said the taller one.

'Right... the diamonds,' said his brother. 'What diamonds?'

'The diamonds from the robbery!' hissed the tall one, keeping his voice low even though he was beginning to lose his temper with his brother, which was unusual for him because he was always in complete control and never did anything that made him look like a plonker. He kept his cool and resisted the temptation to give his brother a clout.

Then the barman brought the drinks - a pint and something weird in a cocktail glass. On the side of the beer glass there was a slice of lemon, apple, orange and a strawberry, accompanied by a colourful little umbrella.

'Funny,' said the tall man, glowering at the barman. 'Good joke. Not smiling, though, am I?'

The barman quickly transferred the decorations to the cocktail glass and turned away.

'Hold on,' said the tall man. 'You look like you probably know pretty much everyone around here.'

'Might do,' said the barman.

'Good,' said the tall man. 'So who would we need to talk to if we had, for instance, a bit of jewellery that we wanted to sell?'

'Depends who's asking,' said the barman.

'I am,' snarled the tall man. 'You probably saw my lips move. Now we might want to do a bit of business, so who's the man?'

The barman looked away, furtively, as though he wasn't talking or saying anything to the tall man, but he was. 'Alf the garden. Railway arches.'

Then he walked away to serve another punter two vodka and tonics and three pints of lager.

'What do we want with a gardener?' asked the shorter man.

'He's not a gardener,' said his brother. 'They just call him Alf the garden because he's a fence. Garden fence, see?'

The smaller brother looked confused, scratched his nose, seemed to like that and slipped his finger inside to have a good rummage around.

2

'So can I see it, then?' he asked finally, flicking whatever he had found up his nostril over to the other side of the bar where it made a tinkly ping as it bounced off a wine glass hanging from a rack and plopped into a bowl of olives.

'See what?' said the tall man.

'The tom we've got. You know - the gold jewels an' suclike.'

'We ain't got any,' said his brother, sipping his pint without leaving any froth or dribble on his top lip. 'I just wanted him to think that we did.'

'Come on,' the little man laughed. 'What sort of brainless twerp is gonna think that we've got a load of hookey tom to shift?'

'You just did,' said his brother. 'The point is, that barman will spread the word. Soon the whole neighbourhood will know that there's a couple of strangers with some goods to trade.'

'Well, anyone who just showed up and started shoutin' his mouth off about that sort of thing would be askin' for trouble. The local villains would think he was a right berk.'

'That's what I'm counting on,' said the tall man. 'So just act naturally.'

A blank look drifted across his brother's face. sometimes that meant he was thinking, but usually not. The tall man often thought that if there was a way that he could somehow squeeze a brain cell into his brother's head, it would be lonely.

A scruffy-looking bloke with dark, greasy hair and a face like a wet Wednesday in Woolwich walked up to the bar.

''Evening,' he said.

'It's lunchtime,' said the tall man.

'Not if you work nights,' said the local.

'You work nights, then?' asked the shorter brother.

'No,' said the local. 'I was just making conversation.'

'I like conversations,' said the tall man. 'You know what I'd really like to talk about?'

'Football?' said the shorter brother. 'Dog racing? No? Motors? Birds? Ah, I give up. I'm useless at this.'

'Buying and selling items of value?' asked the local.

'Right first time,' said the tall man.

'He's too good for me,' sighed his brother, shaking his head. Nothing rattled. Empty containers don't rattle.

'We heard we should pay a visit to Alfie the garden down at the arches,' said the tall man.

'You won't find Alfie down at the arches,' said the local, reaching across the bar to pluck an olive from the bowl.

'Why not?' asked the tall man.

'Because I'm Alfie,' said Alfie, 'and I'm here.' He tossed what looked like an olive into his mouth. For a second, his eyes widened and his face froze like a stopped clock.

THE MASTER AT WORK!

MALLORCA TRIP
★ ★ ★ ★ ★ ★ ★ ★ ★

MEGA FLAKES

Young Artists of the Year 1989

Win a fabulous family holiday staying at a 5-star hotel on the beautiful Spanish Island of Mallorca!

All you have to do is to paint one of your favourite things, fill in the entry form below and send it along with your painting to Megaflakes at the address overleaf.

Competition Entry Form

Name:
Rodney Trotter

Address:
127 Nelson Mandela House
New World Estate
Peckham
London SE15

Date of Birth:
2nd November 1974

Age Group (tick one):
- ☑ Under 15
- ☐ Under13
- nder 11
- nder 9
- nder 7

Title of painting:
Marble Arch At Dawn

Why I chose to paint this subject:
I chose to paint the Marble Arch because it is such an icomic monument and means a lot to me for a lot of reasons. The name is a peach. Marble is good because I used to play marbles and sometimes still do. Arch is also good because it is such a cool shape. It is kind of like an umberellar but you can walk right through it. Also, arches are easy to draw. Much easier than circles. If it had been the Marble Circle, it would have been a non-starter.

Signature of parent or guardian:
Derek Trotter

MEGA FLAKES REF: S6/04

Cassandra made for quite a convincing step-mum!

Rodney is conscripted in to The Groovy Gang!

THE GROOVY GANG

THE GROOVY GANG
Enrolment Form

Full name: Rodney Charlton Trotter

Parent or guardian: Derek Trotter

Room number: 325

I hereby give my permission for _Rodney Trotter_ to participate in all of THE GROOVY GANG activities for the duration of our holiday.

Signed:

Derek Trotter

THE GROOVY GANG
CERTIFICATE OF MERIT
Awarded to

Rodney Trotter

for

Second place in the Groovy Gang Skateboard Derby

THAT'S REALLY GROOVY!

THE GROOVY GANG
CERTIFICATE OF MERIT
Awarded to

Rodney Trotter

for

Finalist in the Groovy Gang Breakdancers Contest

THAT'S REALLY GROOVY!

Trudie – the BROS fan with the hots for Rod!

RODDER'S AWARD-WINNING MANTLEPIECE!

MEGA FLAKES   MEGA FLAKES

Painting Competition

WINNERS ASSEMBLE **HERE**

SOUTHERN CAR SALES

South London's Premiere Car Auction

Lot 557
Cheap to clear!

THE IDEAL 5 CWT VAN FOR THE SMALL TRADER
international

Fast becoming a collectible classic (about the only thing that this car does fast), this 1967 Reliant Regal Supervan III in canary yellow is an ideal bargain buy for the discerning motorist who has always promised himself a nippy little two-seater.

It's cheap to buy and cheap to run - over 70 mpg - and as it's a three-wheeler you only need a motorcycle licence to drive it but on a good day with a following wind you can do up to 50mph!

With a little bit of TLC this old-timer will sail through an MOT. It's got two good tyres and, because the bodywork is fibreglass, no rust.

<u>No reasonable offer refused, so come on - make us an offer!</u>

Sold as seen. Cash only.

No guarantees. No exchanges. No refunds.

OIYIY - Once It's Yours It's Yours

DESIGN SKETCH 1 ★★★★★

Trotters Wares And Trade

Trotters Wares and trade (TWAT) TWAT

TWAT

Abbreviation don't quite have the right effect...

THE IDEAL 5 CWT VAN FOR THE SMALL TRADER

The dependable symbol of trading class!

DESIGN SKETCH 2 ★★★★★

Eye-catching abbreviation!

T.I.T.

TROTTERS INDEPENDENT TRADERS

TIT

TIT

THE IDEAL FOR THE SMA

FABRIQUE BELGIQUE!

DESIGN SKETCH 3 ★★★★★

Dynamic!

Trotters Independent Traders

New York Paris And Peckham

Paris, Peckham New York

PARIS PECKHAM NEW YORK

Like it!

THE IDEAL 5 CWT VAN FOR THE SMALL TRADER

r does fast),

LOWER DEPOSIT FOR SUPERVAN!

You can still buy Reliant's famous 5cwt Supervan III for a deposit of only 20 or 25 per cent with up to three years to pay.

The sturdy, all-purpose Supervan has emerged as better value than ever from the Government's latest economy measures. At the same time, Reliant have given it a more powerful 700cc engine for 1969—without altering Supervan's legendary 65 miles to the gallon.

RELIANT SUPERVAN III £437.10
(no PT applicable.)

Sales Division (WCD) Reliant Motor Company Limited Tamworth Staffordshire

This van comes with its very own Rodney too!

THE FINAL PAINT JOB – FUCKER!

RELIANT REGAL   43

GRANDAD

GRANDAD WAITING FOR RODNEY
TO BRING HIS EMPEROR-BURGER!

```
                              Office of the DOPE
          Peckham Council Maintenance Department
                 Maintenance & Cleansing Depot
                             Canterbury Road
                                     Peckham
                                London SE15


    Edward Kitchener Trotter
    66 Orchard Road
    Peckham
    London SE15


    8 December 1934

    Mr Trotter

    Notice of Dismissal With Immediate Effect

    You are hereby dismissed from your post as a trainee
    painter and decorator with Peckham Council.

    Arriving for work on your first day two hours late
    claiming that you "caught the wrong tram", when there
    is no tram line in the vicinity of the council depot,
    is completely at odds with the fact that you live less
    than ten minutes' walk away.

    Neither does this feebly and clearly fabricated
    fantasy excuse the fact that your first
    day was supposed to be more than three months ago.

    The final straw for your foreman and his supervisor
    came two days later when you were working in the
    council's Executive Dining Room and wallpapered over
    th serving hatch.

    Your employment with the Peckham Council Maintenance
    Department is terminated forthwith. You may apply
    to other council departments for employment but,
    despite your short association with the council,
    your ineptitude has become legendary and it
    is highly unlikely that you will be taken on.


    Yours sincerely

    HChesterfield

    Harold Chesterfield
    Director Of Personnel Employment
```

GRANDAD WITH HIS NO-GOOD SON

NOT ONE OF LIFE'S HARD WORKER'S!

Chalmers Leather Goods Warehouse,
Docklands Road, Peckham, London SE15

18 February 1936
Ted Trotter
66 Orchard Road
Peckham
London SE15

Dear Ted

Don't get me wrong here, Ted, because I think you're a decent enough bloke, but you really landed us in it over that thieving cleaner and I've got to give you the sack, mate.

As a security guard, checking the cleaner's briefcase each night as he left the building was the right thing to do. Fair dos, there was nothing in the case, so you let him go, but it should have struck you as a bit odd that he was leaving with an empty briefcase every night.

And what does a sweeper-up want with a flipping briefcase – especially an expensive leather job like that? The fact that we warehouse and distribute quality leather goods should have told you something.

The Old Bill recovered only a handful of the cases (they reckon 348 went walkies over the course of your time here) and the only fingerprints they could find on them were yours. I told them that you had nothing to do with nicking them but they didn't believe anybody could be that stupid. Until they interviewed you, that is.

The rest of the security team have all been given a right rollocking for letting you work nights instead of us taking turns. The boss reckons that, when you weren't letting people walk off with half the stock, you were probably sound asleep, but I said you wouldn't do that and that the pillow in the office was just to support your bad back when you were sitting in that dodgy chair.

Anyway, I've been told to let you go.

Best of luck

Charlie

C Biggs
Senior Security Officer

GRANDAD WAS A NATURAL WITH A BABY AND A BOTTLE OF GUINNESS!

EYES ONLY   SIS INTERNAL MEMO

FROM: Rt Hon Major Campbell R Robertson, Section Six

TO: Commander Sir Percival H Nelson, Office of the Director

DATE: October 12 1936

Dear Percy

Thought you'd want to know that one of our assets in North Africa has reported two characters who arrived in Tangiers yesterday morning.

I understand that C is taking a keen interest in anything unusual and these two came in as stowaways on a freighter from Southampton. They appear to speak English, but rather badly.

Are you planning on dining at the club this evening.

Cammy

EYES ONLY   SIS INTERNAL MEMO

FROM: Commander Sir Percival H Nelson, Office of the Director

TO: Rt Hon Major Campbell R Robertson, Section Six

DATE: October 13 1936

Dear Cammy

Thanks for the tip. C is very hot on this sort of thing right now. Would you mind awfully asking the local office to keep an eye on them? I believe Harry is out there right now.

Memsahib's in town, so no club tonight. Probably Claridge's again.

Percy

EYES ONLY   SIS INTERNAL MEMO

FROM: Rt Hon Major Campbell R Robertson, Section Six

TO: Commander Sir Percival H Nelson, Office of the Director

DATE: October 14 1936

Dear Percy

Harry reports that our two friends are attempting to join the Foreign Legion. They're not working for Charlie over at Five, are they?

How was Claridge's?

Cammy

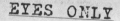

EYES ONLY   **SIS INTERNAL MEMO**

FROM: Commander Sir Percival H Nelson, Office of the Director

TO: Rt Hon Major Campbell R Robertson, Section Six

DATE: October 14 1936

Dear Cammy

These two are definitely not ours or Five's but C is concerned. Best have Harry keep tabs on them.

Claridge's reasonable. Quail's not what it was.

             Percy

EYES ONLY   **SIS INTERNAL MEMO**

FROM: Rt Hon Major Campbell R Robertson, Section Six

TO: Commander Sir Percival H Nelson, Office of the Director

DATE: October 15 1936

Dear Percy

The Tangiers twosome claim to be Norbert 'Nobby' Haig Clarke and Edward 'Ted' Kitchener Trotter. Most certainly false names. They were trying to enlist in the Foreign Legion. Both rejected as unfit for service (I thought the FL chaps took anybody?) and seen negotiating with an Arab well known to Harry.

Trout at the club last night superb with a fine Chablis.

             Cammy

EYES ONLY   **SIS INTERNAL MEMO**

FROM: Commander Sir Percival H Nelson, Office of the Director

TO: Rt Hon Major Campbell R Robertson, Section Six

DATE: October 15 1936

Dear Cammy

C very concerned. Harry's Arab known to be shipping ordnance to anti-fascists in Spain. C believes balloon might go up if Krauts learn Brits involved in gun running to those fighting their Spanish allies. Tell Harry to pick them up.

Chablis with trout? Are you sure?

             Percy

EYES ONLY   **SIS INTERNAL MEMO**

FROM: Rt Hon Major Campbell R Robertson, Section Six

TO: Commander Sir Percival H Nelson, Office of the Director

DATE: October 16 1936

Dear Percy

Too late! Our birds have flown. Will be in Spain with cargo by morning. Harry in pursuit.

Positively decent Chablis. Why not split a bottle this evening? My treat.

             Cammy

EYES ONLY   SIS INTERNAL MEMO

FROM: Commander Sir Percival H Nelson, Office of the Director

TO: Rt Hon Major Campbell R Robertson, Section Six

DATE: October 16 1936

Dear Cammy

C furious. Krauts have been making threats about Brits helping out against their friends. Harry has to get them out.

You were right. Very passable Chablis. Much thanks.

Percy

EYES ONLY   SIS INTERNAL MEMO

FROM: Rt Hon Major Campbell R Robertson, Section Six

TO: Commander Sir Percival H Nelson, Office of the Director

DATE: October 17 1936

Dear Percy

Harry has pulled a few strings. Our friends in Spain on their way home. They claimed to have been told their shipment was "liquorice sticks, false legs, coconuts and castanets."

Off to the Scottish estate for a spot of shooting this weekend.

Cammy

EYES ONLY   SIS INTERNAL MEMO

FROM: Commander Sir Percival H Nelson, Office of the Director

TO: Rt Hon Major Campbell R Robertson, Section Six

DATE: October 17 1936

Dear Cammy

C v. relieved. Krauts still making angry noises. One more slip like this over the next couple of years and C reckons Poland is toast.

Enjoy the shoot. We may all need the practice!

Percy

GRANDAD'S ENEMY – NANA VIOLET!

February 18th 1959

Ted Trotter, you lousy, good-for-nothing old gif!

I know that you've living in Orchard Street with Reg and his family and I haven't the foggiest why poor Joan puts up with you. Well, whether she wants you there or not, they are welcome to you. I don't want to see you back in Deptford any time soon. In fact, I don't want to see you back in Deptford ever again!

I should have seen you for what you are a long time ago – a lazy, work-shy layabout. The only half-decent thing you ever did for me was when you once fixed a bell to the bike I used to cycle to work. That bell was just like you – it never worked either!

The final straw was when I learned about your affair with that trollop Alice Ball. It may have been 15 years ago, but that makes no odds to me. It was my happiest day in years when you walked out of our flat and I was glad to see the back of you.

Don't even dream of ever coming back here. I have taken in a lodger. He is a very nice, clean young man with a steady job. He pays his rent regular as clockwork, and that puts more money in the housekeeping tea caddy than you ever did – but not more than you sneaked out to spend on beer, fags and, no doubt, that slapper Alice Ball!

Good riddance!

Violet

GRANDAD - ALWAYS BRASSIC

BUT RICH WITH KINDNESS

NELSON MANDELA HOUSE'S ORIGINAL TRIFFIC THREE!

The Director General
The BBC
Broadcasting House
London

Ted Trotter
127 Nelson Mandela House
New World Estate
Peckham

Dear DG

I have got a complaint. Actually, I've got quite a few complaints, but let's leave my health out of this. What I want to complain to you about is you doing stupid things. I mean, what do you think you are playing at? What you've done is bang out of order and I ain't seen nothing this daft since Ted Heath announced a three-day working week. I ain't worked three days in one week in my whole life, and I think that most working men in this country are right behind me on that.

But what you have done goes way past that old malarkey. How do you expect ordinary people like me to cope with this sort of thing? I mean, you have ruined my Saturday tea time. What am I supposed to do when you've got the Dukes of Hazzard on one of your channels and the snooker on the other? And to cap it all the ITV lot have got the A Team! How am I supposed to watch em all? We didn't go through the war to be treated like this, you know!

The rest of the week is getting just as bad. If you can't sit down with the blokes from the other side and work out how to make sure that all of the good stuff isn't on all at once, then I don't know what I'll do. The way things are going I'll have to watch three TVs at once!

Yours furiously

Ted Trotter

Edward Kitchener Trotter

Oh Gawd –
Whats he gone and done now!

GRANDAD MULTI-TASKING!

GRANDAD 51

R.C.T. Note to Self   Del Lingo

Del is getting worse. Seems to me that some of what he says nowadays is complete cobblers. Ever since we joined the EEC, he's been using more and more weird foreign-sounding words, usually a bit French.

I used to think he was bi-lingual but when I once said that to him he gave me a Chinese burn and told me that he weren't interested in blokes. Most of the time, I suppose Del knows what he means but this list is so that I can keep a handle on it all. It don't mean that any of it makes any real sense, though.

Rodney working hard towards his DIC.

English:
Hello (to a French person)

Del Lingo:
Au revoir

Well, he's got this totally wrong, ain't he? Au revoir is French for 'goodbye' not 'hello'. I know coz it's about the only thing I remember from French at school apart from when a really tasty French student teacher once came and she was definitely wearing stockings and suspenders, not tights. A lot of pencils was dropped when she was near your desk.

English:
Blimey or strewth

Del Lingo:
Menage a trois

This one's a bit tricky. According to my French dictionary, 'menage' means housekeeping and 'trois' is three. But it ain't three geezers doing a bit of hoovering. It seems to be three people living together like a couple – a treble maybe. So blimey's not too far off the mark.

English:
Certain or without a brussel

Del Lingo:
Oeuf sur la plat

More French, and not in a good way. As far as I can tell, 'oeuf sur la plat' means 'egg on a plate'. Not a clue where Del picked this up but it could be close to 'Sure as eggs is eggs'.

English:
Hello (to a German)

Del Lingo:
Moenchengladbach

Now Moenchengladbach is a town in Germany and also a German footie team. That's where Del probably got this from. He heard it on some football score. He might just as well be saying Leverkusen, or Hertha Berliner, or Blackburn Rovers.

English:
Leave it out, or bloody Nora

Del Lingo:
Plume de ma tante

Back to French again, Del's favourite. From my dictionary, this pans out as 'pen of my auntie'. That don't chime with anything I can think of in real English but you'll hear it from Del if something's happened that's getting on his tits.

English:
Lovely or cushty

Del Lingo:
Pas de Calais

Pas de Calais is an area in northern France near Calais. We've been across the channel to France and Del has heard a few things here and there I guess, but why he calls good things 'Pas de Calais' is beyond me. It's not even that nice there. It's like tasting a nice drop of lager on a hot day, licking your lips and saying, 'Backstreets of Scunthorpe.'

English:
Good on ya, well done

Del Lingo:
Di Stefano

Another very strange one with footie in the background. Di Stefano was an Argie player. He's in my old 'Boys Book of Football Heroes' and he played for Real Madrid in the 1950s. They say he was one of the greatest ever, so I suppose this is a compliment in a way, whether Del knows it or not.

English:
That'll do nicely

Del Lingo:
Fabrique Belgique

He's gone proper European Union with this one. I reckon it means 'Belgian made' but what was ever made in Belgium that was any good? Beer made with strawberries that knocks you sideways after two pints? Waffles? Give me a bacon sarnie any day. Chocolate? Well, theirs is okay but I'd rather have a bar of Fruit an' Nut.

English:
Totally pukka, best of the best

Del Lingo:
Crème de la menthe

I got some help on this one from Maureen down the Nag's Head. She says that Crème de Menthe is a fancy liqueur drink with cream and peppermint. But Maureen also reckons that 'crème de la crème' means 'cream of the cream' – which is used to describe the best of the best. So Del's not too far out on this one, but he's still ballsed it up.

English:
That's the way the cookie crumbles

Del Lingo:
Allemagne dix points

Where he got this from is anybody's guess. Going through my French dictionary again, this comes out as 'Germany ten points'. What's that all about, then? Best guess is It's A Knockout or the Eurovision Song Contest. Either way he's talking twaddle.

MANY OF DEL'S EARLY ENGAGEMENTS ENDED DUE TO BADLY-CHOSEN DELSPEAK!

UNCLE ALBERT
★ ★ ★ ★ ★ ★ ★ ★ ★ ★ ★

THE OLD MAN OF THE SEA

BOOMERANG TROTTER!

THE DAILY HERALD

ONLY 5 CENTS!   PEARL HARBOR EDITION   20th November 1941

PITTSBURGH'S $100,000 FENDER BENDER

USS PITTSBURGH

The pride of the U. S. Navy's Pacific Fleet, the aircraft carrier USS Pittsburgh, has sustained $100,000 damage in a collision with a British destroyer.

The Royal Navy's HMS Peerless was escorting the Pittsburgh through an area of the Pacific yesterday when the incident happened. No US personnel were injured but the damage to the carrier is said to be extensive.

A navy spokesman said, "The Pittsburgh was being escorted through an area that is considered to be a combat zone, although the United States, of course, is not at war with anyone.

"Nevertheless, precautions were taken and the British destroyer was there to screen the Pittsburgh from any potential torpedo attack.

"Ironically, a torpedo would probably have caused less damage than the Peerless."

The Pittsburgh is undergoing temporary repairs at sea before returning to the safety of Pearl Harbor for a full inspection.

The British destroyer is believed to have sunk shortly after the collision.

The U.S. Department of the Navy and the British Admiralty are investigating the incident.

CUBS' HOPE OF EXTENDING WORLD SERIES PAGE 21

AN OLD CIGARETTE CARD THE ANCIENT MARINER KEPT OF HIS OLD TUB

PLAYER'S CIGARETTES

HMS "PEERLESS"

ADMIRALTY TELEGRAM

From: Office of the First Sea Lord, Admiralty HQ, London

To: C-in-C Far East Command, Royal Navy HQ, Singapore

Date: 20 November 1941

Time: 06.37 GMT

WHAT THE HELL HAPPENED TO PEERLESS - STOP - YANKS ARE GOING NUTS - STOP - WHO IS RESPONSIBLE - STOP

YOUNG ALBERT THE BOXING CHAMP! FAMED FOR INVENTING 'THE TROTTER TREMBLER'

ADMIRALTY TELEGRAM

From: C-in-C Far East Command, Royal Navy HQ, Singapore

To: Office of the First Sea Lord, Admiralty HQ, London

Date: 20 November 1941

Time: 09.20 GMT

PEERLESS SET ON COLLISION COURSE BY ABLE SEAMAN ALBERT TROTTER - STOP - CAPTAIN AND BRIDGE OFFICERS RETRIEVED SITUATION ENOUGH TO SAVE PITTSBURGH - STOP - PEERLESS LOST AS A RESULT - STOP

ADMIRALTY TELEGRAM

From: C-in-C Far East Command, Royal Navy HQ, Singapore

To: Office of the First Sea Lord, Admiralty HQ, London

Date: 20 November 1941

Time: 10.59 GMT

COURT MARTIAL PROCEEDINGS UNDERWAY - STOP - TROTTER WILL BE FINED - STOP - TROTTER WILL BE JAILED - STOP - TROTTER WILL BE POSTED TO LAUNDRY DUTY ON THE ISLE OF WIGHT - STOP

ADMIRALTY TELEGRAM

From: Office of the First Sea Lord, Admiralty HQ, London

To: C-in-C Far East Command, Royal Navy HQ, Singapore

Date: 20 November, 1941

Time: 10.40 GMT

YANKS WANT TO KNOW IF WE CAN KEEL HAUL TROTTER - STOP - WE NEED TO THROW THE BOOK AT HIM - STOP

ADMIRALTY TELEGRAM

From: Office of the First Sea Lord, Admiralty HQ, London

To: C-in-C Far East Command, Royal Navy HQ, Singapore

Date: 20 November 1941

Time: 11.30 GMT

GOOD - STOP - SOONER HE IS ON IOW SCRUBBING SOILED SKIVVIES THE BETTER - STOP - THEN WE WILL FIND A SUICIDE MISSION TO SEND HIM ON - STOP

Cell 24
High Security Wing
Changi Prison
Singapore
31 November 1941

The Governor
Changi Prison
Singapore

Dear Gov

I am writing to you to ask if you will apologise
to the top brass and His Majesty for me
messing things up when I was on the old Peerless.

People wonder how I could have made the ship
head straight for that great big Yank job but,
to be fair, I had no idea it was there. I had me
head down staring at the radar screen and I
couldn't make head nor tail of it. It was all blibs
and blobs.

They tell me that I am being shipped back to
blighty tomorrow, so if a one-eyed Chinaman
called Tang comes asking after me and looking
for a few bob what he thinks I owes him over
a small wager on the gee-gees, you can tell him to
sling his hook.

Yours sincerely

Able Seaman
Albert Gladstone Trotter

UNCLE ALBERT WITH COUSIN STAN AND HIS WIFE JEAN AT GRANDAD'S WAKE

THE OLD SEA-DOG DREAMING OF ELSIE PARTRIDGE!

Royal Navy Shore Station HMS Petunia

19 August 1942

Disciplinary Note For The File of:
Able Seaman Albert Gladstone Trotter

Trotter, this is the third of these notes to be
placed in your file and the third time that you have
been disciplined for falling asleep in the laundry
room.
As you must know by now, you are also to be fined a
week's wages. Once more and I'll have you scrubbing
the outside of submarines for the rest of the war,
whether they're on the surface or not!

Lieutenant Ivor Littlejohn Thomas

Lieutenant Ivor Littlejohn Thomas
Station Commander

**ALBERT SAILING FROM HULL
IN 1985, SEA-MAN ONCE MORE!**

**SALUTING SHIPPING OFF THE
MARGATE COAST IN 1989**

The Guard Room
Royal Navy Shore Station
HMS Petunia
Isle of Wight

20 August 1942

Lieutenant Ivor Littlejohn Thomas
Base Commander
Royal Navy Shore Station HMS Petunia
Isle of Wight

Dear Lieutenant Littlejohn Thomas

Please sir, have a heart. If you stop me another
week's wages, then I ain't gonna get paid again until
some time in 1953.

I know that kipping in the laundry room is a bad idea
but, to be fair, it is very warm in there. One minute
you're folding a pile of fresh towels and the next
your sound asleep on em.

How about if I just done a few more days in the
glasshouse instead?

Able Seaman

Albert Gladstone Trotter

The Royal Seamen's Association

INCORPORATED BY ROYAL CHARTER
Charity Registration No 1068707
Patron: **HFR MAJESTY THE QUEEN**
GOSPORT BRANCH, AREA 3 (SOUTHERN FLOTILLA)

The mayer, and George Parker one of uncs former shipmates

Mr Albert Trotter
Flat 127
Nelson Mandela House
Peckham
London SE15 9LP

24th November 2002

Dear Mr. Trotter,

I am writing to invite you to a reunion of your format crewmates involved in the 1944 Mission to Denmark, aboard the HMS Cod.

The reunion is to be held in the village of Ste. Claire de la Chappelle, Normandy. We are hoping for a large attendance of both your formal crew members and local villagers.

If you require help with travel arrangements please contact our Veterans Association on the above number.

We very much look forward to the special event and hope you will be there to join in the occasion.

Your sincerely,

C. Gardener

(Mr C. Gardener)

66 FAREHAM ROAD, GOSPORT, HANTS. PO13 0AG.   Telephone: - 01329 310060.

PROUDLY REPRESENTING UNC
AT THE HMS COD REUNION

STE. CLAIRE DE LA CHAPELLE
OR SHOULD IT BE CALLED: 'TROTTER-VILLE'!

The lovely Marion,
Bunny's cleaning lady

The Funeral of

Albert 'Bunny' Warren

Per Ardua Ad Astra
Through Adversity to the Stars

Order of Service

Hymn:
The Airman's Hymn
(To the tune of Eternal Father Strong to Save)

Eulogy from The Reverend R J Mitchell

Reflective music:
Those Magnificent Men in Their Flying Machines

The Lord's Prayer

Commital

Exit music:
The Dambusters March

Roland (bit of a GIT),
married to Bunny's neice

BUNNY'S SPITFIRE TRIBUTE...

...THE MOMENT WE KNEW WE
WERE AT THE WRONG FUNERAL!

THE LOYAL NAGS HEAD CREW MADE
THE JOURNEY FOR THE SAD DAY

Rodney with the special reef
we ordered for Unc

The Funeral of

Albert Gladstone Trotter

Sailing Into The Sunset

Order of Service

Hymn:
Eternal Father Strong to Save
(For Those in Peril on the Sea)

Eulogy from The Reverend Francis Drake

Reflective music:
What Shall We Do With the Drunken Sailor?

The Lord's Prayer

Commital

Exit music:
We Are Sailing

Alberts urn... and where Damien
hid Cassandra's contraceptive pills!!

PECKHAM HERO REMEMBERS

Remembrance Day is a special and poignant time for everyone, none more so than local war hero Albert Trotter.

Feature by Pamela Liggins

During the Second World War, Albert served with the Royal Navy in the Far East, the Mediterranean and in occupied Europe. He was in action many times and survived a number of sinkings.

"During the war," Albert recalled, "they used to call me Boomerang Trotter because no matter how many ships I was on what got sunk, I always came back. I lost a lot of good mates when HMS Peerless went down. They didn't drown nor nothing, they just didn't want to be me mate any more…

"Them kamikazes was bad. When one of those come crashing down on deck, our whole ship went up and we had to swim for it. We was marooned on a desert island and it turned out that the natives was none too friendly.

"We all legged it along the beach when we saw em coming but the Captain tried to make friends – and he weren't too clever when it came to running on account of his peg leg kept sinking in the sand. We heard they had him for dinner – and not as a guest."

But Albert's adventures in Africa were every bit as incredible as his exploits in the Pacific.

"We all came home via Africa where me and some mates went into the jungle. Somehow I got separated from the rest of them and I came face to face with the biggest lion I had ever seen. Actually, it were the only lion I had ever seen but it was still big as a milk float with teeth like table knives. When he roared at me he opened his mouth so wide I could see all the way down to his tail.

"While he was still roaring, I gave him a swift upper cut to the chin. I was a decent boxer, you know. They used to call my left hand 'Trotter's Trembler'. The old lion was so surprised he didn't know what to do and I was on me toes. I was out of there quicker than you could say spit."

In the Mediterranean, Albert's journey home involved more daring deeds.

"We was on a Greek herring trawler when I saw a torpedo coming straight for us. I turned the ship to face it and it ran right past us, but I kept on going and rammed the trawler right into Jerry's bow. When we was fishing the survivors out of the water, some of them spoke remarkable good English. Some even pretended to be Canadian but we was having none of it and put them ashore on a Greek island somewhere in the Agean."

And Albert's adventures did not end when he eventually got home to England.

"I was stationed on the Isle of Wight. It weren't so bad there but they was just letting me rest there for a while. I was mainly on laundry duty. Before I knew it, though, I had been drafted into a special Commando unit to be parachuted in behind enemy lines in occupied France.

"Why they wanted me there I will never know, but I was pretty good at laundry by then and when you're scared you can get through a lot of underwear I suppose. They did say that none of us was expected to come back alive. Then the war ended while we was out there, so we all did come back alive. Boomerang Trotter, see?"

Quite what the group was up to in France remains classified to this day as Albert uses a veil of modesty to evade questions on the subject, saying simply, "They didn't tell me sod all."

But no one can deny that those keen young men who went off to war demand, as they grow bowed and white-haired with age, our eternal gratitude and deepest respect. ●

The brave crew of HMS Peerless...

...Albert's childhood home, Tobacco Road, sadly now soulless yuppy housing.

The D-Day fleet massed off Isle of Wight, one of Albert's former postings.

Left: Albert as Father Christmas at a recent charity event.

THE DIARY OF JOAN TROTTER (PART 1)

★ ★ ★ ★ ★ ★ ★ ★ ★ ★ ★ ★ ★ ★ ★ ★ ★

THE VILE ERNIE RAYNER

THE RITZ FLEA-PIT!

16 February 1960

I swear I'll swing for that Ernie Rayner one of these days. They warned me about his 'wanderin hands' when I first got the job at The Ritz but it's his rovin eyes that really give me the creeps. It's like he's trying to see right through me usherette's uniform. I'd pack it in if we didn't need the money so bad — and then there's the films. Brigitte Bardot's on in Come Dance With Me. It's all romantic, hot and steamy and passionate — everything I need in my life. Fat chance when I'm stuck with that layabout Reg Trotter. I could be just like Brigitte. Shame they put her name up in lights outside The Ritz as Bridget. It just ain't the same.

DEL BRINGS NYLON CARPETS
TO PECKHAM!

17 February 1960

My Del's a right little grafter, unlike his dad. Del's always got somethin on the go — records straight from America, the latest in beautiful pure nylon carpets and always able to earn a few bob. He brings more in than his dad or his grandad, which ain't difficult. He says he'll buy me a mansion when he's a millionaire, and I reckon he will be one day, too. Until then, I'll just have to keep on working two jobs. At least down the town hall they treat their staff with a bit of respect. I may only be a part-time filing clerk (who sometimes makes the tea) but Mr Johnson treats me like a lady. I wish I could get me name on the list for one of them new high-rise flats I seen on the plans in his office.

HIGH-RISE DREAMS
SERVING TEA TO MR JOHNSON

FREDDIE THE CHARMER
BUYING ME A DRINK

19 February 1960

A funny thing happened tonight down the Nag's Head. A real flash-Harry called Freddie Robdal was in the bar with his strange little mate. I could see him givin me the once over, cheeky sod, but not in the way that old perv Ernie Rayner does. Still, he's got a nerve. Just because he shows up in Peckham in a shiny new Jag and a posh suit he thinks he'll turn all the girls' heads. Well, he might. He's got a certain somethin about him. A bit smart. A bit of charm. A bit dangerous. He ended up back at our house drinking with Reg - somethin about getting Reg to do some work for him. Maybe Freddie Robdal ain't as smart as he makes out! He stole a kiss before he left. Said it was a thank you for me making them all bacon sarnies. I'll have to keep my eye on that one, and there's no great hardship in that — he's quite easy on the eye.

READING 'LOVE IS THE VICTOR'

20 February 1960

Good news at work today. Well, good and bad, really. The good thing is that Rayner has promoted me to Part-time Assistant Manager. The bad news is I'll have to spend more time in his office with him, avoiding his grubby little hands. Still, it means more money.

Would you believe it? Reg and his dad had just scarpered down the Nag's Head with every penny I had in me purse and I was settling down with a cracking good book - Love is the Victor - when who should come knockin at our door but Freddie Robdal. Said he wanted to see Reg but stupid Reg had gone down the pub to see Freddie. Anyway, we had a lovely chat. He told me about his cousin who worked up the Nescafe factory and died when he fell in a vat of coffee powder. I said that was an awful way to die and he said, 'No, it was instant.' I've only just got the joke! He don't half make me laugh, that Freddie. And he has invited me — and Reg — to his house warmin party. What am I gonna wear?

FREDDIE ROBDAL
HANDSOME AND DANGEROUS

BOYCE AUTOMOBILES & CAR HIRE

Boyce Automobiles is your one-stop local expert when it comes to supplying quality motors.

Below are just a few of the outstanding bargains that have been driven out of the Boyce Automobiles showroom recently.

1981 FORD ESCORT 1.3L

£2195

A lovely little runaround with just one careful owner - a grandmother who only ever used the car to pop down the shops and to get to her kung-fu classes - this car is as fresh and straight as the day it left the factory. The sonic blue bodywork is totally unmarked apart from the odd flake of rust and the engine usually starts first time. Runs as smooth as a car at twice the price. £2195

1974 JAGUAR E-TYPE SERIES III 5.3 LITRE V-12 CONVERTIBLE

£25,000

Immaculate in Alpine White with optional whitewall tyres, this is a true driver's car. The E-type is the most beautiful car ever built and just a glimpse of one makes you proud to be British. This car is a real head-turner with all the speed and power you could ever want. You too can feel like a million dollars for just £25,000. (Slight rear end damage but nothing that won't polish out).

When choosing your dream car, make your choice BOYCE!

BOYCE – USED CARS OF DISTINCTION

1987 ROLLS ROYCE SILVER SPIRIT

£70,000

The world's finest automobile, the Rolls Royce just oozes class and luxury. There is no better way to let the world know that you are a man of taste and distinction. The coachwork on this immaculate Roller is finished in Champagne Gold (what else) and the list of extras is as long as your arm. If it tickles your fancy (not one of the extras) you can drive this true thoroughbred away for just £70,000.

1980 FORD CAPRI 2.0 GHIA

£400

Most certainly a car for the connoisseur, this sporty little coupe in emerald green comes with a fully customised, furry tiger skin interior. A fast-appreciating classic car like this is hard to come by nowadays and you won't find a more unique example than this with its contrasting pink wipers and mirrors and enough spotlights on the front to light up Wembley Stadium. Treat yourself to the drive of your life for only £400, or nearest offer.

SOLD

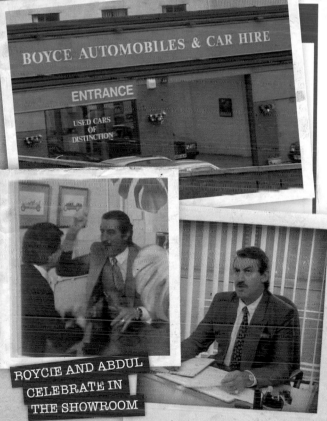

ROYCIE AND ABDUL CELEBRATE IN THE SHOWROOM

The dodgy-dealer himself!

1970 FORD CORTINA MK II CRAYFORD CONVERTIBLE

£50

Very few of these soft-top conversions were made and very few remain in anything approaching the condition that this one is in. With two-tone, black-and-silver coachwork, this is a full four-seat convertible providing open-air motoring for the whole family with the reliability and economy of Ford as an added bonus. Get the wind in your hair for just £50 (no reasonable offer refused).

SOLD

BOYCE AUTOMOBILES & CAR HIRE
SALES UPDATE – MAY 1997

CASSANDRA
★ ★ ★ ★ ★ ★ ★ ★ ★ ★ ★

A GLAM CASS LOOKS ON AS DEL IS AWARDED HIS MEDAL FOR BRAVERY!

Peckham Community College
Business Studies Department

Tutor's Assessment

Student: Cassandra Parry   **Student No:** F73724J

Cassandra has been, in almost every respect, a model student. She is punctual, attentive and studious. Cassandra works diligently and asks pertinent questions during lectures.

It is clear that Cassandra is keen to do well and her understanding of the issues discussed during lectures is apparent through her full participation in the proceedings. She is ambitious, intelligent and capable of expressing herself very well.

There is only one slight cloud hanging over the progress of this exceptional student. Actually, perhaps less of a cloud and more of a pale, mournful shadow. Cassandra appears to have struck up a friendship with a student from the Computer Studies department and he can regularly be seen skulking outside as his classes tend to finish slightly earlier than the Business Studies group.

While it is inevitable that young people will become involved in relationships, in Cassandra's case it appears to have become a real distraction and is detrimental to her studies during the last few minutes of the class – often the most vital few minutes when I am summing up everything that we have been through during the evening. When he is lurking outside, gazing balefully through the glass panel in the classroom door, Cassandra only has eyes for him. When he is not moping around in the corridor, she is constantly glancing across to check for him.

This distraction is ultimately futile and, as with most such relationships, it will ultimately flounder. Cassandra is bright, lively, attractive and charming. There can be no future for her with such a gormless, shambling nincompoop.

Alastair Boothroyd

Alastair Boothroyd
Head of Business Studies

Cass walks to college

Love at first sight!

Rod's middle name 'Charlton' gets a laugh!

A thoughtful Alan and a disapproving Pam!

The Dipstick and Dopey: a perfect match!

Rodney & Cassandra

along with
*Cassandra's parents Alan and Pam Parry
and Rodney's brother Del*

Invite you to join them
to celebrate their marriage at

*Peckham Registry Office,
Castle Street, Peckham*

On January 25th 1989 at 11.00 am

Followed by a knees-up down the Nag's Head!

*RSVP Pam Parry,
7 Queen's Avenue, Blackheath*

Printed by
PARRY
Design and Print, Peckham

A great turn out from the Trotter's and Parry's

They got a good likeness of the plonker Rodders!

Page 12

1989   Marriage solemnized at Peckham Registry Office   in the parish of Peckham

1	2	3	4	5	6	7	8
When married	Name and Surname	Age	Condition	Rank or Profession	Residence at the time of Marriage	Father's Name and Surname	Profession of father
Twentyfifth of January 19 89	Rodney Charlton Trotter	26 years	Bachelor	Trader	Flat 127, Nelson Mandela House, Peckham, London SE15	Reginald Trotter	Porter
	Cassandra Louise Parry	21 years	Spinster	Bank Clerk	7 Queens Avenue, Blakheath	Alan William Parry	Printer

Married in the Peckham Registry Office according to the rites and ceremonies of the Local parish code by Derek Benfield

This Marriage was solemnized between us, { Rodney Charlton Trotter Cassandra Louise Parry } in the presence of us, {

MUM AND GRANDAD WOULD HAVE BEEN SO PROUD

simply red
A Side
45 RPM STEREO
holding back the years
YZ 70
wea

The wedding reception was a very emotional evening

CASSANDRA 71

Peckham Mutual Bank

Serving Peckham Since 1972

Peckham Mutual Bank
176-182 High Street
Peckham
London
SE15

8 December 1992

Mr Derek Trotter
Flat 127
Nelson Mandela House
New World Estate
Peckham
London SE15

Dear Mr Trotter

Re: Business Start-up Loan Arrangement

I am pleased to confirm that the bank is willing to extend a loan to the Peckham Spring Water Company, a division of Trotters Independent Traders, for the purpose of putting this new product into full production.

As you have no existing bank account, a new account has been set up for you, details of which will follow by separate communication. The amount of the loan discussed will be transferred into your new account within the next three working days and you will then be able to access funds in the normal way by issuing cheques or by withdrawing cash at the counter or via one of our autoteller cash machines.

Should you have any queries, please contact me directly and I will be happy to assist.

We wish you every success with your new venture and Peckham Mutual looks forward to a long and fruitful working relationship with TIT.

Yours sincerely

Cassandra Trotter

Cassandra Trotter
Small Business Manager

PECKHAM *Spring Water*

1 litre e

STILL
From an Ancient Natural Source

BOTTLED AT
SOURCE

PECKHAM *Spring Water*

The purest Peckham spring water, drawn from an ancient natural source discovered by returning Crusaders 800 years ago.

The spring is ideally located where prevailing winds and a protected environment together ensure a purity unique among spring waters. Peckham still is a crystal clear spring water, delicious on its own or mixed. The diet conscious will find this pure low sodium spring water irresistible.

TYPICAL COMPOSITION	
Calcium	117
Magnesium	18
Potassium	17
Sodium	28
Chloride	2
Nitrate(an)	2
Sulphat	15

SERVE CHILLED

SWAN'S APPROVED

THANKS TO CASS THE PECKHAM SPRING WAS ABLE TO GO INTO FULL PRODUCTION!

THE PROUD NEW MUM AND DAD

BABY JOAN: A WORK OF ART

Cass said she'd never felt better in all her life

Rodders holds his daughter for the very first time

☆ ☆ ODE TO JOAN ☆

Oh Joan, oh Joan my baby daughter

I love you like a daddy oughter

I love your tiny smile

I love your tiny nose

I love your tiny fingers

I love your tiny toes

Even the smells what make my eyes water

You are the most totally triffic Trotter

R C Trotter,
December 2003

Excerpts from John Sullivan's personal scripts and notes

1981-1983

CAMERA SCRIPT

BBC-1

SUNDAY, 7th JUNE 1981 : T.C.6

<u>Proj. No</u>:   1149/0601

<u>Prog. Ident.No</u>: 1/LLC D211 F

" ONLY FOOLS AND HORSES.... "

by

JOHN SULLIVAN

<u>Episode 1</u>:   "Big Brother"

<u>TX</u>:   T.B.A.

Producer .... RAY BUTT
Director .... MARTIN SHARDLOW
Production Manager .... JANET BONE
A.F.M. .... MANDIE FLETCHER
Production Assistant .... PENNY THOMPSON

T.M.1 .... DON BABBAGE
T.M.2 .... BOB HIGNETT
Sound Supervisor .... MIKE FELTON
Grams Operator .... KEITH BOWDEN
Vision Mixer .... HILARY WEST
Floor Assistant .... MARTIN DENNIS

Designer .... TONY SNOADEN
Costume Designer .... PHOEBE DE GAYE
Make-Up Artist .... PAULINE COX

Properties Buyer .... CHRIS FERRIDAY

Crew .... 8 - RON PEVERALL

<u>SCHEDULE</u>:

10.30 - 13.00	Camera Rehearsal (with TK-22/16mm)
	     (+ TK-40/35mm & VT.22 for Titles transfer -
	     VT available 10.30-12.15 only)

13.00 - 14.00	LUNCH

14.00 - 18.30	Camera Rehearsal (with TK-22/16mm)
	     (+ TK-40/35mm 14.00-15.30 & 17.00-18.30
	     + VT.22 14.00-18.30 for playback)

18.30 - 19.30	DINNER
19.30 - 20.00	Sound & Vision Line-Up (+ Audience Warm-Up)

<u>20.00 - 22.00</u>	<u>RECORD</u> - On VT.3, VT.4 + V.H.S. cassette
	
	     (with film from TK-22/16mm
	     + Opening titles from TK-40/35mm or
	     VT.22 - Spool No:)

(<u>Note</u>: Material for TV sets to be on U-matic cassettes)

"ONLY FOOLS AND HORSES...." No. 1 - "Big Brother"

/STANDBY VT-22 or TK-40/

/RUN VT-22 or TK-40/

1.   VT-22 or TK-40
    Spool No:
       or
    35mm S.O.F.
	SIGNATURE TUNE ON VT
	OR S.O.F.

Opening Titles montage
of animated stills
and captions

Dur: 00'37"

S/I Sub-Title Slide:

    "BIG BROTHER"

MIX TO:

(3 next)

CAMS. 1A, 2A, 3A, 4A

2.	3	M.L.S. ROD – PAN R. TO GRANDAD & TVs	SCENE 1. STUDIO.

INT. DAY. THE TROTTERS LOUNGE

THE ROOM SHOULD REFLECT THEIR
STYLE OF BUSINESS. NOTHING IS
PERMANENT. THE SETTEE AND TWO
ARMCHAIRS ARE FROM THREE SEPARATE
SUITES. (THE OTHER PIECES BEING
USED AS MAKE-WEIGHTS IN VARIOUS
PAST SWOPS)

THERE ARE THREE TV SETS, ONE
COLOUR, ONE BLACK AND WHITE AND
THE OTHER HAS ITS BACK OFF AWAITING
REPAIR.

THERE ARE A COUPLE OF STEREO
MUSIC CENTRES STANDING ONE ON
TOP OF THE OTHER.

VARIOUS VIDEO GAMES, TALKING
CHESS GAMES ETC., LITTER THE ROOM.

THEIR PHONE IS ONE OF THE
ORNATE 1920's TYPE WITH SEPARATE
EAR-PIECE (ON AN ALABASTER BASE)

THE DECOR IS CLEAN BUT GAUDY.
DOZENS OF CLASHING PATTERNS. IT
SHOULD LOOK LIKE THE START OF A
BAD TRIP.

ROD IS LYING ON SETTEE CHECKING
THE COMPANY ACCOUNTS WITH THE HELP
OF A POCKET CALCULATOR.

ONLY FOOLS AND HORSES....

STARRING DAVID JASON AND NICHOLAS LYNDHURST
WRITTEN BY JOHN SULLIVAN

- 2 -

(Shot 2 on 3)

GRANDAD IS WATCHING THE
TWO T.V's WHICH ARE SHOWING
A FILM FEATURING A BLACK ACTOR.
(WE SHOULD NEVER BE CLOSE ENOUGH
TO DISTINGUISH WHO THE ACTOR IS)

GRANDAD:
That Sidney Potter's a good

actor, ain he Rodney?   He

was marvellous in Guess Who's

Coming to Dinner.

ROD:
Yeah, knockout, Grandad! ...

3.   4   M.C.U. ROD   (REACTS)   Sidney Potter?

4.   1   M.S. GRANDAD

GRANDAD:
Yeah, you know him, always

plays the black fella.

5.   2   M.S. ROD

ROD:
It's Sidney Poitier.

(1 next)

(Shot 5 on 2)

_____

6.   1   M.S. GRANDAD

                                    GRANDAD:
                                    It's Potter!

                                    ROD:
                                    It's Poitier.

                                    GRANDAD:
                                    It's Potter.

_____

7.   2   M.S. ROD

                                    ROD:
                                    It's bloody Poitier I'm telling

                                    you.

_____

8.   3   M.L.S. GRANDAD
         TO INCLUDE U/S DOOR

                                    GRANDAD:
         (4 next)   And I'm telling you it's bloody

                                    Potter.

                                    - 4 -

(Shot 8 on 3)

DEL ENTERS

DEL:
You two at it again, are you?

---

9. 4   WIDE 2-SHOT
         ROD/DEL

ROD:
Del, how would you pronounce
that fellas name on the telly?
Sidney Poitier or Sidney Potter?

DEL:
Personally I'd pronounce it
Harry Belafonte, but you two
please yourselves.

ROD:
You daft old sod it was Harry
Belafonte all along.

---

10. 1   M.S. GRANDAD -
          PAN HIM TO TVs

GRANDAD:
Well I wondered why Sidney Potter
kept bursting into song...I don't
like Harry Belafonte. (SWITCHES
T.V.'S OFF OR TO ANOTHER CHANNEL)

(2 next)

- 5 -

BBC LIGHT ENTERTAINMENT, TELEVISION

Programme Ident. No:

1/LLC D216 B

REHEARSAL SCRIPT

JOHN SULLIVAN

" ONLY FOOLS AND HORSES.... "

by

JOHN SULLIVAN

Episode 6: "The Russians Are Coming!"

Producer/Director .... RAY BUTT
P.M. .... JANET BONE
A.F.M. .... MANDIE FLETCHER
P.A. .... PENNY THOMPSON

Designer .... TONY SNOADEN
Costume Designer .... PHOEBE DE GAYE
Make-Up Artist .... PAULINE COX

Properties Buyer .... CHRIS FERRIDAY

The sending of this script does not constitute an offer of a contract for any part therein.

SCENE 2.   STUDIO

INT.   DAY.   THE TROTTERS LOUNGE.

SCATTERED AROUND THE ROOM IN
SMALL PILES ARE THE BOXES
FROM THE SITE.

ROD IS LAID OUT ON SETEE
READING A PAMPHLET AND SOME
OTHER PAPERWORK.

DEL, SWEATING AND EXHAUSTED,
ENTERS CARRYING ANOTHER BOX.

GRANDAD FOLLOWS HIM IN 'ROLLING'
ONE OF THE BOXES.

GRANDAD:
That's the lot, Del Boy.

(HE GOES TO PLACE THE BOX ON

TOP OF AN EXISITING PILE)

DEL:
No Grandad,   We've got three

tons here so spread it over

a wide area, otherwise we'll

be having tea with Mrs. Obooko

downstairs!

                /cont'd....

            - 7 -

DEL: (cont'd...)
I hope we're not disturbing
you with all this humping and
sweating, Rodney!

ROD:
No don't mind me, you carry on.

DEL:
Lazy little bark.

GRANDAD:
Why didn't we just put it all
in the garage?

DEL:
Because Grandad, we have got
some very good friends living
in this estate, and if our very
good friends were to see us
putting three ton of lead in
our garage, they'd nick it
faster that you could say twenty
one pound an hundredweight.
O.K.? ...

/cont'd...

- 8 -

DEL: (cont'd...)
(TO ROD)   What's that you're
reading?   Another dirty book
is it?   My God Rodney, you've
got a mind like a plain brown
envelope....I'll have a look
at it when you've finished.

ROD:
It's some paperwork I found in
one of these boxes...D'you
know what we've got here?

DEL:
We have got three lovely ton
of lead that's what we've got
here.

ROD:
No it's more than that...That
factory was producing pre-
fabricated structures right?
Garden sheds, bungalows etc.
This was one of its experimental

/cont'd...

- 9 -

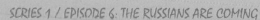

ROD: (cont'd...)
lines - it's a do-it-yourself

nuclear fall-out shelter!

DEL:
A do-it-yourself nucl...

DEL AND GRANDAD BURST INTO
LAUGHTER.

DEL
What a wally!

ROD:
(OFFENDED) It is. Honest.

DEL: Give over Rodney!
a do-it-yourself nuclear
bleedin'- fall-out shelter
I've never heard nuffing like
it!

DEL:
(TO GRANDAD) ~~You didn't leave~~

~~any glue around for him to sniff,~~

~~did you?~~

ROD:
Look at this pamphlet. (THEN

UNFOLDS A LARGE PIECE OF PAPER)

And here's the plans, tells you

how to build it.

-10-

DEL, STILL LAUGHING, LOOKS
AT PLANS.   STOPS LAUGHING.

DEL:
He's right as well, it is a
fall-out shelter. Perhaps it's
worth more than we thought.

ROD:
You can't sell it.

DEL:
You don't want to put money on
that, do you?   What do you
suggest we do with it? Build
it?

ROD:
Yes!

DEL:
Leave off, Rodney.   Who
wants a nuclear fall-out
shelter?

-11-

ROD:
These days, everyone!

GRANDAD:
we ~~·~~Shouldn't have too much
this
trouble flogging ~~it then~~!

ROD:
~~Wait a minute, just think about~~
it
~~this, think about it, will you.~~
~~This could be a life or death~~
~~decision. International~~
~~relations are strained - every-~~
~~where you look in the world there~~
~~conflict.~~   Do you realise how
close we came to world war three
over Cuba, Vietnam, Afghanistan
and Poland?   All it needs is
a little rumble in the Middle
East and the missiles will be
flying!   And what have we got
in Britain to combat the might
of the Soviet Union? / Three
jump-jets and a strongly worded
letter to the Russian Ambassador!

- 12 -

DEL:
You don't know what ~~we've~~ [this country]
got up ~~our~~ [it] sleeve, Rodney.
Did you know that we had a
device that can keep track of
the movements of every Russian
nuclear submarine?   They
can't keep track on ours.

ROD:
We've only got one.

DEL:
Have we?

ROD:
I think so.

DEL:
Well - anyway, they don't know
where it is....I sometimes wonder
if we do!

- 13 -

BBC LIGHT ENTERTAINMENT, TELEVISION   Programme Ident. No:

REHEARSAL SCRIPT   1/LLC E073 S

Production Office: 7022 T.C.
                  Ext. 2153/8

JOHN SULLIVAN
(Ol' Red Eyes is Back)

" ONLY FOOLS AND HORSES..... "

(2nd Series)

by

JOHN SULLIVAN

Episode 3:   "A Losing Streak"

Producer/Director .... RAY BUTT
Production Managers .... JANET BONE
                                   SUE BYSH
Production Assistant .... PENNY THOMPSON
A.F.M. .... TONY DOW

Designer .... ANDY DIMOND
Assistant .... JOHN HOLLAND
Costume Designer .... ANUSHIA NIERADZIK
Make-Up Artist .... SHAUNNA HARRISON

Properties Buyer .... ROGER WILLIAMS

The sending of this script does not constitute an offer
of a contract for any part therein.

"ONLY FOOLS AND HORSES....." (2nd Series)

EPISODE 3 - "A Losing Streak"

RUNNING ORDER

PAGE	SCENE/SET	CAST	CAMS/SOUND	SHOTS
1.	OPENING TITLES Stills montage & film	Del/Rod Grandad		
1-9	1. STUDIO: INT. TROTTERS' LOUNGE - DAY	Del/Rod Grandad		
10-28	2. STUDIO: INT. NAG'S HEAD PUB - DAY	Del/Rod Trigger/Boycie Barmaid Customer Paddy Customers - Extras		
29-39	3. STUDIO: INT. TROTTERS' LOUNGE - EVENING	Del/Rod Grandad Trigger Boycie		
40-62	4. STUDIO: INT. TROTTERS' LOUNGE - NIGHT	Del/Rod Grandad Trigger Boycie		
62.	CLOSING TITLES			

50   50
50   100
100   100
        100

Boycie   ← 100
Del   *50 + 150 = 200
Boycie   500 + 100
Del   100 + 200 = 300
Boycie   200 + 1000

BOYCIE:
Not good enough me old mate is it?
(SCOOPS THE KITTY IN) Well I suppose
that's the end of the game is it?
(PLACING THE MONEY IN BRIEFCASE)
Shame, I was just getting into me
stride.

GRANDAD:
(QUIETLY TO TRIGGER) He knows more
card tricks than Paul Daniels don't he!

TRIGGER:
(QUIETLY) D'you reckon he's switching
'em?

GRANDAD:
Course he's switching 'em! He's done
you two up like a couple of kippers.

BOYCIE:
Well I'll bid you adieu.

ROD, FILLED WITH HATE, MOVES TOWARDS
BOYCIE AGGRESSIVELY.

ROD:
D'you know what you are Boycie?

BOYCIE, NOW COLD AND THREATENING,
TURNS AND FACES ROD.

BOYCIE:
What's that Rodney?

-39-

ROD, SENSING THAT BOYCIE MIGHT PUNCH
HIM ALL ROUND THE ROOM, REACTS.

ROD:
(BOTTLE GONE) You're double lucky
that's what you are.

BOYCIE:
No no Rodney, it's skill my son skill!
When it comes to cards I'm an artist.

GRANDAD:
You ought to be with all the pictures
you pulled out!

BOYCIE:
Some shall be born artists - others
shall be born wallies - that is the
way of things.

DEL:
(CAN TAKE NO MORE OF THESE INSULTS)
~~Right Boycie~~. Hang about! Boycie!

DEL GOES TO SIDEBOARD AND REMOVES ONE
OF THE DRAWERS. HE KNEELS DOWN AND
REACHES INSIDE THE GAP. HE TEARS
SOMETHING FROM THE BACK OF SIDEBOARD
AND PRODUCES A YELLOWING ENVELOPE.
HE OPENES ENVELOPE TO REVEAL A WAD
OF NOTES. (THEY SHOULD BE NOTES THAT
WERE IN CIRCULATION DURING THE MID-60'S)

DEL:
I've got five hundred quid here that
says the game aint over!

-40-

a bon droit (With justice)

a coeur ouvert (with open heart – with the utmost candour)

a centre-coeur (against one's will – against the grain)

a haute voix (in a loud voice – loudly; openly)

air distingue (a distinguished appearance)

a l'outrance (to the utmost; with tooth and nail)

amour-propre (self-love)

apres moi le deluge (after me the deluge – posterity is no concern of mine)

a propos de rien (Concerning nothing in particular)

argent comptant (hard cash – ready money)

arriere-pensee (mental reservation – ulterior motive)

a tort et a travers (at random – without discretion)

autres temps, autres moeurs (other times, other customs)

avant-coureur (a forerunner; a precursor)

a votre sante (to your health)

ballon d'essai (a trial balloon – to test opinion)

beche-de-mer (a sea-slug – used in Chinese cookery)

beton-arme (reinforced concrete)

billet-doux (a love-letter)

bonnes nouvelles (good news)

boutonniere (a button-hole)

brevet d'invention (a patent)

a la brochette (grilled on a skewer)

cafe noir (black coffee)

canape d'anchois (anchovy on toast)

catalogue raisonne (a catalogue of books)

cela va sans dire (it goes without saying)

c'est-a-dire (that is to say)

c'est egal (it's equal)

c'est le premier pas qui coute (it's the first step that counts)

chapelle ardente (where a dead person lies in state)

chevaux de frise (Friesland horses)

comme il faut (correct; proper)

conseil d'etat (a council of state)

de haut en bas (from top to bottom)

dernier ressort (at the last moment)

droit des gens (international law)

entre nous (between ourselves)

faute de mieux (for want of something)

feu de joie (a bonfire)

force majeure (superior force)

fortune de la guerre (the fortunes of war)

frappe (iced)

gens de monde (people of fashion)

grace a dieu (thanks to god)

haricote verts (French beans)

homme d'affaires (a businessman)

jour de fete (a saints day)

lapin saute (stewed rabbit)

mauvais sujet (a bad character)

pour comble de bonheur (the height of happiness)

pour passer le temps (to pass the time away)

que voulez–vous (what would you?

tete de veau (Cookery: a calf's head)

tout de suite (at once)

ventre a terre (at full speed)

vogue la galere (come what may)

ONLY FOOLS

Ideas for 3rd series.

The Cottage — (The Trotters go fishing and borrow Monkey Harris's cottage. Only to find they are fogged in and an escaped lunatic is on the loose. Face at the window — "Doctor" calls (turns out to be the loony. Del ends up playing phantom snooker with him).

Diamonds Are For Heather.

Del meets Heather at a Spanish night at the Nags Head. Del goes to court with her to swear that they are to marry soon, thus enabling Heather to keep her small son. During a shopping trip they see a diamond necklace and a man's watch in a jewellers. Del believes all the stuff about the wedding — a ready made family. Rodney discovers that Heather thought Del's oath in court was just a favour. It ends in the Nags Head on French night. Del has been given the elbow but kept the necklace.

Bingo

Bingo – an ex-convict from Birmingham meets Del and Rod in the Nags Head. Bingo is trying to find lodgings as the company he is supposed to deliver his 'juggernaut-load to is strike bound. He stays at the Trotters flat for £15 a night bed and grandads breakfast. Bingo is violently determined to go straight.

One of Dels friends (charlie) calls Del for help as he has been told that the police are about to raid him. He needs a way to take away his illicit stock.

Del and Rod drag Bingo out of a local bingo parlour. DEL (CALLS) "Bingo!".

CALLER:
House has been called.

When they get to Charlies and open Bingos juggernaut they find it is empty. Charlie stole it.

Charlie:
You can have a crate of whisky for 50pence

DEL:
(LAYS DOWN A FIVER) I'll have ten!

Arabian ~~that~~ Nights

Del and Rod are offered a
well paid - no tax - job in Arabia
by Monkey Harris.
~~They finally~~ turn it down for
grandad. We discover that Grandad
wanted them to go as he planned to
move Mrs Someone (the old lady from
downstairs) into the flat.

The Outing.
~~The~~ Jolly Boys Outing to ~~South~~
Southend.

Heroes

Del and Rod catch a young skinhead
who is mugging an old lady from the
estate. After the conviction they become
paranoid that the skinheads friends are
after them. One night they are chased
by other skinheads. They end up
taking refuge in the old ladies flat
whereupon she allows the skinheads to enter.
They turn out to be her grandsons who
were merely trying to thank Del for
what he did. Del ends up selling them
a consignment of Chinese (race).

ONLY FOOLS AND HORSES

Stick a pony in me pocket
I'll fetch the suitcase from the van
Cause if you want the best 'uns
And you don't ask questions
Then brother I'm your man

Where it all comes from
Is a mystery
It's like the changing of the seasons
And the tides of the sea
But heres the one thats
driving me berserk
Why do only fools and horses work

La la lala - la la la la la (etc)

HOOKY STREET

We've got some
half priced cracked ice
And miles and miles of carpet tiles
TV's, deep freeze
and David Bowie LP's
Pool games, gold chains,
wosnames
And at a push
Some Trevor Francis track-suites
From a mush in Shepherds
Bush, Bush, Bush,
Bush, Bush, Bush, Bush, Bush

No income tax, no VAT
No money back, no guarantee
Black or white, rich or broke
We'll cut prices at a stroke

God bless Hooky Street
Viva Hooky Street
Long live Hooky Street
C'est magnifique Hooky Street
Magnifique Hooky Street

Lyrics by John Sullivan

MY LOVE AND QUEEN OF PUCKER, RAQUEL...
SHE CAN TELL A LIE THE MOMENT IT LEAVES MY LIPS!

Cabaret Night at the

TALK OF THE TOWN

●●●●●●●○ HATFIELD

KEVIN
THE TALKING COLLIE

(who once bit Hughie Green on TV's **Opportunity Knocks!**)

Singing sensation
★★**SANDY SHORE**★★

Impersonations galore with
MARK YEARWOOD
The Man of a Thousand Voices

International Nowegian dance troupe
THE TRONDHEIM TILLER GIRLS

Plus
the up-and-coming musical duo
★**DOUBLE CREAM**★
Featuring **Gillian Woolcott** and **Raquel Turner**

---

10 July 1989

THE MARDIS GRAS CLUB
MARGATE'S PREMIER ENTERTAINMENT VENUE

ALL THIS WEEK!

GERRY N' JIM
The Cheeky Cockney Geezers play the hits of **Chas n' Dave**!

PLUS! Marvel at the incredible magic of
THE GREAT RAMONDO
and Raquel

Limited menu • Disco 10.00pm til Midnight • First drink free

TECHNOMATCH

COMPUTER DATING AGENCY

Sign up for just 3 months and if we can't match you with your soul mate, you can have a full refund! *

Gonna put that on your floppy disc or what?

Fill in the form below and we will process your details through Cupid, our love-match computer system, to find your ideal partner!

Name: Derek Duval

Age: 42

Sex: Powerfully, yet passionately and caringly, Male

Height: Above average with charismatic presence

Hair colour: Dark, romantic, lustrous

Eye colour: Alluring

Profession: Business entrepreneur dealing with imports and exports via company offices in New York, Paris and Peckham.

Interests: High finance and international economics, naturally, but all work and no play makes Jack a dull boy, as they say, and dull is not what Derek Duval is all about. I unwind after a hard day's international trading by enjoying fine wine, listening to proper music and enjoying haute cuisine. Any lucky girl who goes on a date with me is guaranteed a pukka, sit-down steak dinner.

I thought she'd gone and stood me up!

Would most like to meet: Somebody handy, and I mean near at hand, not an all-in wrestler! I lead a busy life and don't want to be driving my executive saloon here there and everywhere of an evening. Ideally, I want a bit of a looker, not too young but a bird who's kept herself in fairly good nick. Not too tarty – I'm looking for a touch of class. I don't want some old slapper who doesn't know a Bowjerlay Noovow from a bottle of brown ale.

* Refund in the form of vouchers for a further 3 months' membership. No cash alternative.

A PUCKER PARKING SPACE!

TECHNOMATCH

COMPUTER DATING AGENCY

Sign up for just 3 months and if we can't match you with your soul mate, you can have a full refund! *

Fill in the form below and we will process your details through Cupid, our love-match computer system, to find your ideal partner!

Name: Raquel Turner

Age: 30

Sex: Female

Height: 5ft 4in

Hair colour: Dark

Eye colour: Dark

Profession: Singer, actress, cabaret artiste and 'musical greetings performer.'

Interests: Movies, music and theatre. My favourite film is Brief Encounter. I also love dancing and take tap and modern dance classes as well as drama tuition.

Would most like to meet: A man who enjoys the arts and has a tender side. I would like to meet a caring, honest individual who will appreciate me for what I am and who will be a genuine companion. I do have ambitions for my career as an entertainer and he would have to be prepared to support me in trying to achieve my goals. I want someone who will make me feel empowered so that I can wake up each morning and think, 'Let's get to work — this time next year I'm going to be a star!'

Refund in the form of vouchers for a further 3 months' membership. No cash alternative.

CHRIS STANTON: THE AGENT WHO PUT US TOGETHER

A nervous first meeting...

...and off on our first date, at the Hilton!

The Great
RAMONDO
and Raquel

*One performance
to really forget...*

Curriculum Vitae

RAQUEL TURNER

Actress, Singer, Dancer, Entertainer

Address: Flat 127, Nelson Mandela House, New World Estate, Peckham, London SE15
Vital statistics: Height 5ft 4in; Hair dark; Eyes dark; Weight 8½ stone

EXPERIENCE

Television
Speaking part in one episode of *Dr Who* in the 1970s. I was Lizard Person No 4. The opportunity was there to expand on this with further TV roles but I became married and my then husband (now divorced) persuaded me to give it all up and I put my career on hold for nine years.

Theatre
Rosalind in Shakespeare's *As You Like It*. This was a touring production playing to schools in inner cities but I had to back out when I fell pregnant. It was not thought that, no matter how modern the schools we visited, Rosalind's romance with Orlando would be taken seriously if Rosalind was clearly five or six months gone.

Musicals
I toured the United States, including shows in Atlantic City, Miami and New Orleans, with *My Fair Lady*, playing a flower seller.

Musical Greetings Performer
This was a job that involved interacting with the audience in small venues and taught me how to command the attention of an entire room; how to sing in close proximity to the audience; how to wear a variety of costumes and how to remove the costumes elegantly in time to the music without missing a note. There performances are also sometimes referred to as 'strippergrams'.

Dancer
I toured with a revue show in the Middle East, although the tour was rather limited due to the dancer's costumes being banned in certain venues and, try as you might, you can't cut many good moves when you're hidden away in a burka.

Popular singing
I formed a duo with a friend when we were teenagers and we sang in a number of clubs but the act split up when she ran off with the manager of the Beachfront Nightclub in Southend and three week's takings from the safe. I also sang with Tony Angelino at the Starlight Rooms in Peckham, although Tony's inability to pronounce the letter 'R' turned our rendition of the ballad 'Crying' into more of a comedy number. In fact, Tony's renditions of almost everything turned us into a comedy act. I suppose that me being heavily pregnant at this point didn't help.

Cabaret
I played a season with The Great Ramondo as his assistant at the Mardi Gras Club in Margate. If nothing else, it taught me how many different ways there are to hide live pigeons in your clothing.

References available on request.
Roles requiring nudity, scenes of a sexual nature or energetic acrobatics are unlikely to be considered.

Stevenson & Co, Solicitors & Notaries Public, Peckham

Tel: 0207 139364392   **Fax:** 0207 139364393

Stevenson & Co
Solicitors
12 Dockyards Way
Peckham
London SE15

24 January 1991

Raquel Turner
Flat 127
Nelson Mandela House
New World Estate
Peckham
London SE15

Re: Divorce proceedings

Dear Ms Turner

Today we received a visit from a Mr Derek Edward Trotter who claims to be your 'significant other'. Mr Trotter informed us that you were in a 'right two and eight' following a recent encounter with your estranged husband, Mr Roy Slater.

Mr Trotter further intimated that Mr Slater would be willing to consider what is termed a 'clean break' separation as he has found himself in what appears to be an awkward situation, described by Mr Trotter as Mr Slater having to 'do one sharpish if he doesn't want to end up back in the slammer.'

While Mr Trotter advised us that you would want to 'make it a quickie' because you were 'up the duff' there are still some formalities that we need to go through with you. I would be pleased if you could give me a call at your earliest opportunity to arrange to come in and see me.

Please also thank Mr Trotter for paying for the services of Stevenson & Co in advance. This is quite unusual, as is payment in cash, but you need not worry at all about that side of things. I would also appreciate it if you could ask Mr Trotter to get in touch as the Lithuanian answering machine that he sold us is not working properly.

When you call, it's probably best not to bother trying to leave a message.

Yours sincerely

Robert Stevenson

Robert Stevenson
Stevenson & Co

SLATER AND RAQUEL'S WEDDING DAY!

105

DAMIEN

★ ★ ★ ★ ★

HE'S A LAD AINT HE!

MY LITTLE TROUBLE-MAKER

Peckham General Hospital
Muamar Gaddafi Road • Peckham • London SE15

The Dorothy Squires Maternity Wing

Raquel Turner
Flat 127
Nelson Mandela House
New World Estate
Peckham
London SE15

21 February 1991

Dear Ms Turner

Congratulations on the birth of your son. We hope that little Damien is thriving now that you have him at home. Your local health visitor will be in touch with you soon, if he or she has not already done so.

I must apologise for the attitude of some of our staff when you were in the Maternity Wing. I understand that the delivery team did their usual efficient and professional job but that some of the aftercare staff refused to be left alone in the room with your son because they found him 'disturbing' and said he was 'creeping them out.' Their silly superstitions were further inflamed by the baby's uncle pointing out that Damien was born under a full moon, checking his head for numbers and making the sign of the cross every time his name is mentioned.

This is not normal behaviour for our staff and you should feel nothing but pride in your beautiful baby boy. Damien is a perfectly normal, healthy baby, no matter what anyone says.

I wish you, Damien and your family every happiness for the future.

Yours sincerely

Dr Steven Horlicks

Dr Steven Horlicks
Hospital Administrator

A PROUD MOMENT
WELCOMING DAMIEN TO THE FAMILY

THIS IS WHAT ITS ALL ABOUT

RCT – Damien – is he normal?

I am really startin to wonder about Damien. He is not like any other baby I've ever known. Okay, so I ain't been around many babies. Last one I really saw up close was Boycie's nipper, Tyler, and Boycie was a bit scared of him. Before that it was Megan who I used to sit next to in the fourth form. She brought her sprog into school one day and it looked like a prune with limbs. Just like Megan really. So maybe all babies are a bit strange. But Damien takes the biscuit.

These notes are to help me keep tabs on some of the weird stuff that happens around him, and for anyone to read should anything happen to me, because I'm seriously worried about the way that kid keeps givin me the evil eye.

The heart attack

Once, when I was alone with him in the living room, he looked up from his cot and stared straight at me like he was trying to bore holes in me with his eyes. I had a scary, wet feeling in my chest, like my heart was being turned to mush. When I took my jacket off later, a biro had burst in my pocket and left an ink stain all over my shirt. And the stain was in the shape of a black bat.

The milk incident

I was pouring milk in my tea and Del was pacing the floor with Damien. Then he let out a horrible, threatening, growly noise. Del reckoned it was time for a nappy change and went off to find Raquel, but when I sipped my tea, the milk had gone off....

The numbers

I am convinced that we will one day find the number 666 – the number of the beast – on Damien somewhere and Del might know something about that. He got very cagey when I asked him if there was any numbers on Damien anywhere and just said, 'Leave it out, Rodders! Numbers? He's a baby, not a bleedin' raffle prize!'

The grip

Damien was asleep in his cot but I could see that the blanket was a bit close to his face so I reached in to move it. Suddenly those big dark eyes were open and his hand shot up from under the blanket. He gripped my finger really tight – you might almost think he had a strength that was more than human. Only five days later I had a hang nail on that finger.

The voices

He has started making noises like he is tryin to talk, but what he's sayin' ain't English and it don't sound much like any other human language, either. Is what we are hearin some kind of communication from another realm?

Synchronized snoring

Albert was asleep in his chair ☐ nothing unusual about that. Damien was asleep in his cot ☐ nothing unusual about that either. They could both kip for England the amount of shut-eye they put in. What was spooky was the snoring. They was both snoring in time. Damien was copying Albert so that it sounded like some kind of satanic stereo. Very strange.

ROD AND CASS WERE GODPARENTS
AT DAMIEN'S CHRISTENING IN 1991...

...AND SLEEP-OVERS
AT HIS UNCLES FLAT!

Damien loved
to play war!

Always had time for his Dad

Peckham Lane Primary School
Peckham Lane, London, SE15

End of Term Report, June 1999

Name: Damien Derek Trotter   Year 3

Teacher: Mrs Pendleton

General behaviour:

Damien has a very colourful turn of phrase for an eight-year-old, although we have now persuaded him not to react with 'Bloody Nora!' when his marked work is returned to him in class. Some of the other children had started to copy him, thinking that this was an acceptable reaction to the teacher's marks. Next term we hope to wean him off 'Stone me!' as well. Damien is a talkative little chap but now seems to understand that what the teacher has to say is usually more relevant than his own opinions. He accepted this with a rather enigmatic expression 'Bonnet de douche'.

Attendance:

Damien has yet to complete a full week but at least once he is in school he now tends to remain with us for the whole day.

Attainment:

Damien struggles to come to terms with some of the more abstract concepts in mathematics but he has a very good grasp of Arithmetic, particularly when it comes to adding sums of money. He was also able to explain to his teacher how a betting slip worked and how to calculate your winnings from the 'odds'.

His reading and writing are not as well advanced as we would like and, while we have encouraged him to look at magazines and periodicals, we would rather he did not persist in bringing the *Racing Post* to school. Neither is it appropriate for him to be offering other boys pages from magazines that are not appropriate for their age group at prices he describes as 'Knock-down bargain basement deal of the century.'

MARTIN LUTHER KING COMPREHENSIVE
Community Education in the Heart of Peckham

22 May 2003

Mr Derek Trotter
Flat 127
Nelson Mandela House
New World Estate
Peckham
London SE15

Dear Mr Trotter

Sadly, this is not the first time that I have had to write to you about your son, Damien.

There was the incident with the overheating Korean calculators; there was the distribution of falsified parental letters claiming everything from asthma to encephalitis (spelt with an 'f') to get pupils out of PE; there was the batch of fountain pens that could shoot ink up to a distance of five metres.

Damien's latest enterprise is selling kebabs in the playground at lunchtime now that the school meal service 'has gone all Jamie Oliver'. The school menu has been specially developed to give the pupils the kind of nutrition that growing bodies need. Damien must not sell foodstuffs on school premises as it seriously undermines our efforts.

It is not right that Damien should treat the school as some kind of marketplace and his fellow pupils as 'punters' as he puts it.

We will take a very dim view of any further moves by Damien to use his time at the school as an opportunity to make money.

As usual, he is excluded for one week.

Yours sincerely

James Thripplethwait

James Thripplethwait
Headmaster

Never far away from his catapult!

THE BOY WATCHES THE BOX
WITH HIS MUM AND AUNTIE

Chip off the old block –
Damien enjoys a cigar!

Flat 127
Nelson Mandela House
New World Estate
Peckham
London SE15

25 May 2003

James Thripplethwaite
Headmaster
Martin Luther King Comprehensive
Dockside Road
Peckham
London SE15

Dear Mr Thripplethwaite

What are you like? Here we are in the dog-eat-dog world of the 21st century and you are complaining about a fine young man showing a bit of initiative and entreprenoorial flare. That's the sort of thing you should be teaching in schools these days, not chuckin out the poor sods who try their hand at a bit of duckin an divin.

If you don't encourage youngsters like Damien to have a go at doing a bit of business, then where will our future captains of industry and commerce come from? Where will we find the next Rupert Burdock or Charles Scratchi?

Damien will be back at school again next week. By the way, I tried phoning you earlier but I couldn't leave a message because it says your answering machine is full. As it happens, I might be able to help you out there.

I have in stock a small number of top-quality, state-of-the art answering machines just in from Brazil. There are lots of different machines on the market these days but these really are the dogs. In John Lewis or Currys they would be asking you 200 notes for these beauties but I can let you have one for just £35.99. If you're interested, just give me a bell – but not the school bell or you won't know whether you're coming or going! Ha-ha!

Bonjour

Derek E Trotter

Derek E Trotter

THE POSTER WHICH DON THE OLD LANDLORD
HUNG IN THE NAGS HEAD, ADVERTISING THE EVENT

MARGATE MESSENGER

STILL ONLY **2d**

July 2nd 1960

JEWELLER RAIDED

Burglars blew open the safe of a local jeweller yesterday and escaped with gems worth up to £5,000.

Butler & Co, Baltic Road

One of Margate's best-known family-run jewellers, Butler & Co in Baltic Road, was closed for the Bank Holiday when the burglars struck in a dramatic raid that involved blowing open the safe.

Mr Gerald Butler, whose father and grandfather ran the business before him, is mystified about how the burglars got in.

"All of our doors have the best locks that money can buy," said Mr Butler, "but they couldn't keep these people out. The safe door was blown to pieces along with half the room. I don't know how they got out alive."

Mr Butler believes that the burglars were professional jewel thieves. "They knew what they were after, all right," he said. "We lost some of our finest pieces – diamond necklaces, a diamond and emerald brooch that was of outstanding quality and one item in particular that was quite exquisite.

"It was a gold ring set with a large

One of the treasures now missing

ruby surrounded by a cluster of diamonds."

According to the police, the high-value items may be difficult for the thieves to sell intact, and they may be broken up with the gems sold separately from their gold and silver settings. Mr Butler thinks that they may be right.

"Some of the pieces, especially the ruby ring, would be difficult to sell intact as they are so recognisable. They are more valuable as they are, but they will be easier for the thieves to sell if they break them down. Such a shame."

Butler & Co will be open for business as usual tomorrow and Mr Butler was at pains to reassure any of his clients who had ordered engagement or wedding rings that they will not be inconvenienced in any way.

"Butler & Co will not disappoint any of our regular customers and we will be open for business again tomorrow. The war couldn't shut us down and neither will this."

Police are appealing for witnesses.

FREDDIE THE FROG LOOKING SHADY...

SINGING ON THE BUS DOWN!

ALBIE MOPES AT THE HALFWAY HOUSE!

COCKTAILS À LA DEL
★ ★ ★ ★ ★ ★ ★ ★ ★ ★ ★ ★ ★

Note to Rodders

Pay attention, bruv an you might learn somethin here about how to be a bit suave, a bit sophisticated and a bit debondare. Naturally, I have no need of a cocktail list as I have already committed all of these to my phonogramic memory, but if I ever need you to whip up a couple of refreshing bevvies, these are the best recipes.

All of these have been specially created to cater to the discerning palate of the international jet set, so don't go wastin the good stuff on any old bow-wow you pick up down the Down By The Riverside Club.

Serve each of these masterpieces up in the fanciest glass you can find – none of your half pint lager mugs.

DYNAMIC AND TASTY!

Caribbean Stallion

What can I say? Pas de Calais, this one's really the dogs. It ain't for the faint of heart, though. There's a shedload of booze goes into this, so don't even attempt it unless you're prepared to get totally legless. And whatever you do don't drive after havin one of these . . . for a couple of days.

* 1 shot Tequila
* 1 shot Coconut Rum
* 1 shot Creme de Menthe
* A smidgin of Campari
* The merest suggestion of Angostura Bitters
* Top that up with fresh grapefruit juice
* Shake it – do not stir!
* Pour slowly over broken ice
* Garnish with a slice of orange, a slice of lime, occasional seasonal fruits.
* Top it all off with a decorative umbrella, two translucent straws and wallop – a Caribbean Stallion.

Tequila Sunset

This is one of me all-time favourites. Nothin impresses the ladies more than a man with a gold chain that says, 'I'm not short of a bob or two'; a suit that says, 'I've got more style and taste than Gerald Harper on a night out with Carol Lagerfeld'; and a Tequila Sunset in his hand.

* 1 shot Tequila
* A splash of Grenadine
* 1 shot Cherry Brandy
* Orange juice
* Pour into a glass with more ice in it than the Titanic and then dribble the orange juice in to top it all up.
* Garnish with a slice of orange and a couple of Mary Chinese cherries.
* Add the usual straws, swizzley sticks and Bob's your uncle!

Pina Colada

This one's so good that they even wrote a song about it. Come on, you know how it goes – If you like Pina Colada, an getting sloshed like a drain . . . or somethin like that. Anyway, this one's a belter if you're feelin a bit Tom Dick the morning after a heavy night on the sauce because it's really smooth and soothing.

* 1 shot Bacardi
* A big slosh of Creme de Coconut
* A handful of pineapple chunks – the tinned fruit, not them rock-hard sweets
* Put the whole lot in a blender with some crushed ice
* Whizz it all up until it's smooth, but don't forget to screw the lid on or you'll be runnin around trying to catch the drips off the ceiling

The blender bit is sometimes not such a good idea when you've got one of them mornin after heads as it gets a bit noisy. Be brave. Remember – He who dares, wins!

Banana Surprise

This one really gets the girls going. It's a well-known fact that Banana Liqueur is a powerful amfrodizzyac and a couple of these puts em right in the mood for a romantic interlude.

* 1 shot Banana Liqueur
* 1 shot Amaretto
* 1 shot Southern Comfort
* Top up with Pineapple Juice
* Pour the whole lot onto crushed ice and shake
* Tip it into a glass, peel a banana and slip it in there, hanging over the edge.

If that banana peekin out from under the umbrellas and straws don't give them ideas, then it just ain't your night, Rodders – as bleedin usual!

Singapore Sling

Well it don't come much more exotic than this, does it? This really is a tightener for the jet set as it comes from Singapore, which is in Hong Kong. This is a cocktail for top stars like your Jimmy Depps and your Robert Bedfords.

* 1 shot Gin
* 1 glug of Cherry Brandy
* 1 dribble of Lemon Juice
* 1 slosh of Creme de Cassis
* 1 drop of Grenadine

Bung it all in a glass and top it up with soda water Maybe add a slight touch of lime juice if you're feeling adventurous. Garnish with lime, strawberry, lemon plus the usual umbrellas, straws, etc

Don't take the name to heart. Sip gently, don't sling it down your neck!

MIKE FROM THE NAG HEAD IS A MASTER OF THE BANANA SURPRISE!

Rusty Nail

This is a real man's cocktail and tells everyone who sees you with one of these babyies in your hand that you are a man who can really hold his licker. So don't try it, Rodders. You stick to your usual cocktail – half a layer and lime.

* 1 shot Drambuie
* 1 shot Whisky
* Add ice, give it a stir and hold on to your hat!

PECKHAM **MUSICAL** **PMT** **TIMES**

November 1988

55p

KYLIE MINOGUE LOVES PMT!

GUNS N' ROSES SAY 'WELCOME TO THE JUNGLE'

RAQUEL TURNER IN CONCERT

Win a chance to meet Milli Vanilli!

My beautiful significant other...

...with the voice of an angel

RAQUEL IN CONCERT
Peckham's Own Songbird Live

By Rob Charlesworth

Raquel Turner took to the stage at the Down By The Riverside Club for a one-night-only appearance that left the audience wondering why she was there for one night. In fact, many were wondering why she was there at all.

Is this geezer some kind of smart-arse?

It's not that Raquel can't sing – actually she has the making of a perfectly good voice – but the choice of songs for her performance were way off beam.

Cheeky git! I chose some of them songs!

Some of the songs were completely wrong for her character and her voice. What on earth was she thinking about, for example, when she included 'Old Shep' in her repertoire?

It was me what chose that one – it's the best song ever!

Raquel Turner is no Tina Turner, but she can belt out a good ballad when it suits her vocal range. Listening to her, you get the impression that her range is limited not by a lack of skill or talent, but by her lack of confidence. She was understandably nervous when she first walked out on stage, but once she had got past 'Old Shep' as an opening number, she began to settle into a more predictable routine.

That audience was putty in her hands once she'd knocked em bandy with Old Shep!

When she hit some rhythm with more up-beat numbers like Abba's 'Dancing Queen', Raquel was able to show that she could move quite nicely. She has a few dance steps that she carries off with commendable elegance and the distraction of dancing only caused her to forget the words once.

Raquel's dancing even prompted a degree of audience participation. Although most members of the audience remained seated at their tables, tucking into their chicken-in-a-basket, Raquel looked hugely uncomfortable when one gentleman took to dancing in front of the stage. His dancing was actually more like a cross between a limp, a lunge and a limbo. How he managed it without spilling the huge cocktail he was holding is anybody's guess.

Practice, skill and a touch of le ne sequins, mate, that's how I done it!

As the dancer was ejected from the premises, Raquel really got into her stride, putting real grit into her rendition of Bonnie Tyler's 'It's A Heartache'. With the audience under control, Raquel relaxed with a touching version of Stevie Wonder's 'You Are The Sunshine of My Life' and Carly Simon's 'Nobody Does It Better'.

Both sung for me after I sneaked back in through the basement.

Overall, it was a creditable performance where Raquel showed that, with a little more stage experience and a little more polish, she has the potential to become Peckham's own superstar! *RC*

Well, at least he got that right.

TRIGGER

★ ★ ★ ★ ★ ★ ★

TRIGGER PROPPING UP
THE BAR OF THE NAGS HEAD

CERTIFIED COPY OF AN ENTRY OF BIRTH

GIVEN AT THE GENERAL REGISTER OFFICE, LONDON

Application Number ___CO12298847___

REGISTRATION DISTRICT _Peckham_

___1946___ BIRTH in the Sub-district of ___Mitcham___ in the _London Borough of Merton_

Columns: –

1 When and Where born	2 Name, if any	3 Sex	4 Name and Surname of father	5 Name, surname and maiden surname of mother	6 Occupation of father	7 Signature, description and residence of informant	8 When registered	9 Signature of registrar
12 May 1946 Back seat of a Vauxhall in Mitcham	Colin Arthur	Boy	Some soldiers	Elsie Ann Ball	Fighting	Arthur Ball Grandfather Sloane Street, Peckham	14 May 1946	Cedric Martin

Given in the GENERAL REGISTER OFFICE, under the Seal of the said Office, the __18th day__ day of __May__ 19__46__

NX **74205** This certificate is issued in pursuance of the Births and Deaths Registration Act 1953. Section 31 provides that an certified copy of an entry purporting to be sealed or stamped with the seal of the General Register Office shall be received as evidence of birth.

TRIG ON HIS LAMBRETTA IN 1962

THE PECKHAM PACK HIT THE TOWN, TRIG SECOND RIGHT

Peckham Echo

22 May 1946

PECKHAM'S BACK SEAT BABY

A Peckham mother has given birth to a healthy baby boy on the back seat of an abandoned Vauxhall in Mitcham.

Mrs Elsie Ball was said to be confused and tired when she sat down in the car to take a rest in the early hours of Tuesday morning. When she started to give birth, passers-by heard her cries and rushed to her aid.

The baby was delivered by a nurse, Miss Carol O'Brien who had been waiting for a bus to work when she heard Mrs Ball call for help. 'The poor woman,' said Miss O'Brien. 'She was in a bit of a state and didn't really know where she was or what was going on. I will never forget the look on her face when I put the baby in her arms. She was horrified.'

Mrs Ball, whose husband died in France during the war when a rack of wine fell on him in the cellar he was guarding, was too emotional to be interviewed but her father, Mr Arthur Ball, is glad to have her back home.

"It's been a trying time," said Mr Ball, a roadsweeper for Peckham Council Cleansing Department, "but Elsie and the nipper are both doing fine. We will be eternally grateful

The patch of waste ground in question

to everyone who helped our daughter when she went into labour."

Asked what his daughter was doing in an abandoned car on a patch of waste ground at 5 o'clock in the morning, Mr Ball could not give a clear answer.

SOUTH LONDON & LOCAL, VOCAL WEEKLY

Peckham Echo

Thursday September 17th 1996

OLD BROOM SWEEPS BEST

A Peckham roadsweeper has been given a medal at the annual Peckham Council Community Awards Ceremony.

Colin Ball, with Councillor Murray

Colin Ball, affectionately known to everyone as 'Trigger', was awarded his medal for outstanding service to the community. The presentation was made by Councillor Murray.

"I think it is safe to say that Peckham would not be the same without dedicated workers like Mr Ball,' said Councillor Murray. "This man is out sweeping the gutter come rain, hail or shine, keeping Peckham's streets clean and safe.

"Peckham needs more outstanding citizens like Mr Ball. He has even been using the same broom for more than 20 years."

Trigger was thrilled with his medal. "I've never won nothing in me whole life," he said. "I like to do a good job, but it ain't always easy. Sometimes it can take me a whole week to do a decent day's work.

"I like to do everything just the way my grandad showed me. He was a roadsweeper before me and he taught me everything I know, and quite a lot of the things what he knowed, too."

Asked what changes he had seen in his job over the years, Trigger said, "Well, there's the traffic. It just gets worse and worse every year. Sometime in the mornin the queue of cars, buses and lorries stretches back for miles behind me."

And what about that famous long-lasting broom that he's been using for two decades. "Yup," said Trigger, "They say a new brooms sweeps clean, but an old broom sweeps best. I still use the same old broom – and it's only

had seventeen new heads and fourteen new handles....."

When he was called upon to sum up his feelings about the award, Trigger became quite emotional, dabbing away a tear. "Well," he said, "this is a great honour for me. I can't really describe exactly what if feels like. It's a bit like when you accidentally pick up someone else's pint at the bar and it's got more left in it than yours did – a real result.

"But how do I feel deep down? It's kind of like my mate Dave would say......cosmic."

TRIG ON THE JOB!

Trig wearing his medal with pride!

Final Request of Arthur Ball

Dear Colin

If you are reading this now then I am gone, but I am also glad because it means you finally learned to read.

Since your mother died, you have been far more like a son to me than a grandson, and I was proud to see you take up the broom to carry on the family trade. Treading the same streets with brush, shovel and cart as your old granddad did.

And I was proud of your two fine, long legs which carried you round the streets far better than my one good leg and the bit of an old sideboard I had to use as peg leg. I will never forgive them for taking away my proper artificial leg. How could they class it as an 'offensive weapon' just because I whacked a couple of mouthy gits with it now and again.

I am proud of you, son, but also know that you will do one last thing for me. You see, during the war, while I was off fighting in France (which is where I left my own leg), that dirty little scumbag Ted Trotter came sniffing round your grandma. Alice was lonely and frightened and Trotter took advantage of that. No fighting in France or anywhere else for him, of course. He was unfit for duty due to an allergic reaction to loud bangs.

So that cowardly little git made a play for your grandma, while his own wife, Rose, was out working in a factory helping the war effort.

He's kept well out of my way ever since I found out, but he can't avoid me forever – and he can't get away from me now that I've kicked the bucket. If you ask anyone around here if there's a family that can call on their Romany ancestry to weave a little gipsy magic, they'll tell you, 'Balls!'

And that's what I want you to do for me, Colin. Make sure old Trotter gets the message that I have cursed him from beyond the grave!

Then have a nice life. And remember never to put your working gloves on the wrong hands or your shirt on before your vest.

Love
Granddad

TRIG'S GRANDMA'S WAKE BROUGHT US TO ARTHUR'S HOUSE

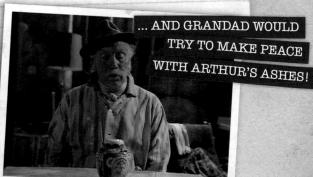

... AND GRANDAD WOULD TRY TO MAKE PEACE WITH ARTHUR'S ASHES!

Trig out with a bird he met from a dating agency...

and romance at Christmas!

Dear Colin

I see you are back at work this morning.

I wondered what happened to you on Friday night after we had our little chat in the afternoon. Now I hear that you went away for the weekend on your own.

Did you not realise that when I suggested going away for the weekend, I had it in mind that we would both go TOGETHER?

Clearly not. I thought that your gormless nature was all a bit of an act. Seems I was wrong about that. You really are as thick as you look.

Well you needn't come moping around my desk any more. This weekend I went out with Archie from Accounts. He has a Ducatti. Now we're engaged.

Goodbye

Linda.

TRIGGER'S DOS AND DON'TS

★ ★ ★ ★ ★ ★ ★ ★ ★ ★ ★ ★ ★ ★

Trigger, a word in your shell-like.

As a mate, I have given you the benefit of my advice on a number of occasions, but you still keep making the same old boo-boos. If it's just that you struggle to remember what you should and shouldn't be doin, here's a solution. Why don't you have a flick through these cards and memorise what's on em?

Then have a flick through again this afternoon and memorise em again. If you remember. Okay, I'll see you in the Nag's Head. Your round.

Del

DO try to remember that Dave is actually called <u>Rodney</u>.

DO find a new chat-up line. 'Hello darlin', where have you been all my life?' is well out of date.

DO get it into your head that the bird you fancied in Dr Shifargo was Julie Christie, not Agatha Christie.

DO act normal on your next blind date. You don't have to wear dark glasses like Stevie Wonder or Roy Norbinson.

DO tell people that you was Head Boy at Dockside Secondary Modern, cos you was. You was NOT Headmaster.

DON'T steal pork pies from across the bar at the Nag's Head, deny doing it and then eat one in front of the guvnor.

TRIG LOVED SHOWING OFF HIS MEDAL!

DON'T announce to the entire pub that you are 'just poppin round your sister's to sort out an alibi for next week', whatever you might be gettin up to next week.

DON'T let Roy Slater fit you up for stealing 3,000 Green Shield stamps ever again, even if you did get an electric blanket and a toaster when you came out of jail.

DON'T give names to your teeth – you know you'll only get upset when the dentist pulls em out.

DON'T show up for work wearing your best blue suit. You are a road sweeper, not a stockbroker. And the donkey jacket is for work, not the disco.

Trigger did over the Nag's Head fag machine once!

PLAY IT NICE AND COOL TRIG, NICE AND COOL!

MUSICAL DOORBELLS GOING FOR A SONG!

Tired of a dreary old doorbell that's been ding-donging away for so long that it makes you want to punch the Avon Lady? Get yourself kitted out with the very latest in musical door chimes.

These high-quality musical chimes have a tune to suit every taste with 36 different national anthems on offer.

In the store that will never be beaten on price, you'll pay £36 for these beauties – that's a nicker an anthem. But we will beat them on price and, for a limited period only, we will include batteries and fitting – all for only £13.99!

Call TITco on Peckham **1405 67900**

WINTER SPORTS MADNESS!

When you're out in the snowy ski sloped of the French Alps, the Swiss Toblerones or the Italian Sodomites, you need kosher kit to keep out the cold. The latest in high-performance ski wear as worn by Olympic Gold Medallist Alberto Tombola and Roger Moore as 007 in *The Spy Who Loved Me*. In ever-popular high visibility colours for safety, these jackets will make sure you can be seen in an Arctic blizzard, an Alpine avalanche or even the fog on Peckham Rye. Reinforced with pure fibre-glass padding and lined in high-quality natural nylon, the garments are hand made by cold weather experts in Fiji. Totally windproof, waterproof and repels tea or lager stains. Stay warm and stay safe for only £35!

Just £35!

Call TITco on Peckham **1405 67900**

BROADCAST STANDARD VIDEO RECORDERS

When the professionals record telly on tape, they uoc the latest Matzuki video recorders with the ever-popular Betamax system. Manufactured in Formosa, the Matzuki has state-of-the-art built in computers.

When David Attenborrow's somewhere up the Zambesi, he don't want to risk missing Panorama, does he? So he bungs a tape in before he packs his insect spray and his jar of Branston Pickle (you can't get that where he's going) and sets his Matzuki to record all his favourites while he's away. Now you can do the same – tape all your stuff while you're off on holiday and never miss an episode, all for just £50.

Call TITco on Peckham **1405 67900**

(May include inappropriate operating instructions)

FINE CHINA SALE

They have to call it China, but this exquisite porcelain actually comes from North Korea.

Ideal for cat lovers or collectors of hand-crafted China, these beautiful oriental cat figurines make marvellous ornaments but can also be used as jewellery boxes and revolve while playing 'How Much Is That Doggy In The Window?'

You'll be seeing these on Antiques Roadshow before long, so get your claws into a bargain that will leave you purring like a pussy cat - £1.25 each or two for a fiver.

Just £1.25!

Call TITco on Peckham **1405 67900**

STEREO SOUNDS FOR YOUR CAR

When it comes to in-car entertainment, these Musta F80 Radio Cassettes are hot-hot-hot stuff!

Features multiple presets, synthesised tuners, digital scan, auto reverse, graphic equaliser, MW, FM, VHF, LCD, RMS, B&Q and ICI. Comes complete with not one, but two quadrophonic speakers.

Free Kylie Minogue LP for the first few lucky customers!

Only £10.99!

Call TITco on Peckham **1405 67900**

ADAPTABLE CYCLE HEAD GEAR

You can't be too safe when you're out on your bike and every cyclist knows that a helmet is an essential accessory.

As worn by professional cyclist Stan Boardman, these are the ultimate in cycle hats. They can even be easily adapted to make cycle turbans for safety conscious Sikhs.

Just £9.99!

Call TITco on Peckham **1405 67900**

RUGGED CAMCORDERS FOR FAMILY MOVIES

These amazing camcorders are the most robust examples on the market. Made in Kazakhstan, they are very popular with the Russian Army. They are manufactured to withstand the worst conditions on earth, so they're just the thing for filming all those special moments during a week at Butlins or your granny's wedding in Scunthorpe.

Relive your most memorable moments in full colour.

(Can only be used with Russian video tapes)

Call TITco on Peckham **1405 67900**

DELSPEAK (PART 2)
★ ★ ★ ★ ★ ★ ★ ★ ★ ★ ★ ★ ★

R.C.T. Note to Self   Del Lingo

It has got to the stage where even I don't know what Del's on about half the time. He's not only talkin cobblers with all his mixed-up foreign malarkey – he's talkin fluent cobblers. We had some French tourists on the market yesterday and Del was givin them his best Inspector Clouseau. They thought he was Welsh and had a whip-round to buy him a bus ticket back to Cardiff.

Del always knows what he means, I think, but there's no way he'll ever speak French or any other language. Let's face it, he's still strugglin with English. Just in case I have to remind him what he means, though, I need these notes to keep me right.

Some of the work at college was very challenging!

English:
Goodbye, tara or laters

Del Lingo:
Bon jour

Couldn't be more wrong, although I reckon 'Bon' means 'good' in French so he's got one bit right by accident. Actually, if 'jour' means 'day', then 'Bon jour' actually means 'good day' which is posh for 'goodbye', innit? I'll have to stop thinkin about that before I persuade meself that it's the French have got it all wrong!

English:
Certainly or no problem

Del Lingo:
Mange tout

This is a complete mystery. I've looked up mangetout and it's them green bean pea-pod whatsits. I can't even work out how you'd do it using rhyming slang. It just don't make sense.

English:
Nothing ventured, nothing gained

Del Lingo:
Boeuf a la mode

I got it from Sid, who used to run a caff, so he should know about food, that 'Boeuf a la mode' is beef boiled in red wine. Del doesn't know what he's talkin about here. Mind you, I've eaten in Sid's place, so why should I think he knows what he's talkin about either?

English:
Without a doubt

Del Lingo:
Bonnet de douche

According to my old French phrase book, 'Bonnet de douche' means 'hat of the shower'. I'm guessin that's a shower cap like women wear to stop their hair gettin wet. Del must have water on the brain to think he can get away with that one.

English:
Without a word of a lie or straight up

Del Lingo:
Petit Suisse

I worked out that 'Petit Suisse' probably means 'small person from Switzerland'. How does that translate to 'I'm being honest'? After all, that Sepp Blatter bloke was a small person from Switzerland, weren't he?

AMAZINGLY RAQUEL SEEMED
TO BE INITIALLY IMPRESSED
BY DEL'S LINGO!

English:
For Pete's sake

Del Lingo:
Potpourri

No, it don't even work as some kind of a swearword. Potpourri is just something old, dried up and smelly. Sounds a bit like Grandad or Albert. Anyway, Del might as well stamp his foot and say 'Rose petals!' or 'Lavender stems!' That might ruin his reputation as a lady's man...

English:
That's the way it is, or stop moanin and get on with it

Del Lingo:
La bonne vie

Been flickin through the French dictionary again and 'La bonne vie' seems to come out as 'The Good Life'. Well, I suppose it is 'the good life' for Del when he tells me to get on and do all the work, so maybe he ain't too far off on this one!

English:
That'll do nicely

Del Lingo:
Tres bien ensemble

Mickey Pearce always reckoned that this had something to do with three birds havin a bit of slap an tickle together. If it was, he'd have filmed it. In fact, it seems to mean 'very well together'. So maybe Mickey wasn't far off the mark, and neither is Del. Quelle surprise.

English:
Hello (to a Dutchman)

Del Lingo:
Ajax

Now I don't know whether Del got this from watchin the footie (Ajax the football club from Amsterdam) or watchin the ads (Ajax the floor cleaner) but I suppose Ajax sounds a bit like 'hiya' so maybe he does think it means hello in Dutch. Still makes him look a prat but fortunately we don't meet too many people from Holland.

English:
Perfect or pukka

Del Lingo:
Chasse de forme

I'm stumped with this one. Best I can come up with from the French book is 'shape of the hunt'. And if that's some kind of rhyming slang I'm not even gonna hazard a guess at it....

I ALWAYS USED TO TELL EVERYONE
NEW TO THE AREA - BOYCIE IS A TIGHT GIT!

Dockside Secondary Modern School
Peckham, London, SE15

School Report **June 1960**

Name: <u>Herman Terrance Aubrey Boyce</u>

Form: <u>Class 4c</u>

Head Teacher's comments:

Herman is, overall, a diligent pupil, although appears to be easily led astray by some of his more rowdy contemporaries. He is capable of expressing himself very well in class and can, I am assured by one of his teachers (who served in the Royal Army Service Corps during the war), swear quite fluently in German. And Italian. And Spanish. Sadly, his mastery of foreign profanities does not reflect an aptitude for languages in general, even English.

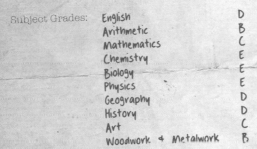

Subject Grades:

Subject	Grade
English	D
Arithmetic	C
Mathematics	E
Chemistry	E
Biology	E
Physics	D
Geography	D
History	D
Art	C
Woodwork & Metalwork	B

Head Teacher's Comments on Grades:

Herman would do better if he concentrated more on work and less on moneymaking schemes. His relative proficiency in metalwork was in evidence when he sawed up a metal cupboard and sold the pieces to younger pupils as 'Genuine bits of Adolf Hitler's personal Heinkel.' There is, it would seem, an aspiring businessman in there somewhere, looking to emerge. Hopefully he will emerge before Herman finds himself looking at a barred window in Wormwood Scrubs.

BOYCIE GOT THE DODGY MOTOR DEALS BUG EARLY AT ALBERTO'S AUTOS

BOYCIE AND ME DURING THE MATING SEASON OF 1960!

Luftwaffe High Command
POW Repatriation Unit
Herman Goering Hause
Berlin
Germany

19 May 1949

Colonel Harold Secombe
Commanding Offier
Royal Military Police
Prisoner Processing Centre
Wellington Barracks
Aldershot
Hampshire

Dear Colonel

For some times now (it is since 1943, not less) we are trying to locate the
Luftwaffe Officer Oberleutnant Gunther Herman Langsteiger. We are knowing
for certain sure that he is crashing over England und that he is surviving
the crash as we have the witnesses of the eye.

Oberleutnant Langsteiger's Messerschmitt was hit by ein lucky shot from a
Spitfire und was diving towards the cliffs at Dover, which are not as white
as you English are thinking. His aircraft was involved in what you call ein
'near miss', but we know in German as ein 'Effinnearcrappenselfen', with
ein other Messerschmitt who has following him down und sees him crashing und
getting out of his pitcock to light a nice cigar. He was then captured by
two very old soldiers with the white hair like Santa.

When he is being made a prisoner, we believe that he is being sent out
to work in some places. This is not normal for ein German officer und we
are thinking that this was his chance to be escaping. Instead, we are
hearing that he is living with ein Englishwoman in Lewisham. This is most
distressing for wife in Stuttgart.

Can we please be having Oberleutnant Langsteiger back as soon as is
possibility?

Much thanking you

Fritz von Pfeiferwurst

Colonel Fritz von Pfeiferwurst

Royal Military Police
Prisoner Processing Centre

Luftwaffe High Command
POW Repatriation Unit
Herman Goering Hause
Berlin
Germany

27 May 1949

Dear Colonel Pfeiferwurst

Thank you for your enquiry about Oberleutnant Langsteiger. I can only apologise for the delay in tracking down this officer, but we did take rather a lot of your lot prisoner. There were so many of your Messerschmitts shot down by our Spitfires that there was a danger that areas of outstanding natural beauty like the White Cliffs of Dover (which are unlike anything along the shore of northern Europe) were in danger of looking like a Luftwaffe scrapyard.

Oberleutnant Langsteiger appears to have settled in rather well with the Boyce family and the local community in Lewisham and protested at great length when a few of our chaps went to visit him early one morning. Seems he's not used to getting up much before 10.00 hours, so kicking his front door in at 04.00 hours came as something of a shock to him. And the woman who thought she was his wife. And their young son.

Still, he's on his way back to you now under escort, so the real Frau Langsteiger will, no doubt, give him a warm Teutonic welcome when he gets home.

Yours sincerely

Colonel H Secombe

Colonel H Secombe
Royal Military Police

GRAND ORIENT OF PECKHAM AND CAMBERWELL
Hear, See, Be Stumm

Councillor Alan Stanhope
Mayor of Lambeth
Lambeth Town Hall
Lambeth Walk
Lambeth
London SW2

Greetings, Brother Stanhope

We believe that you are aware of the circumstances in which a friend and possible future brother of the Grand Orient, Aubrey Boyce now finds himself.

While we are aware that you did not play a direct part in his incarceration, we must now call upon you, and others, to do all in your power to effect his release from Wormwood Scrubs immediately.

We must remind you that Junior Steward Boyce is entitled to any and all help that we can give him, regardless of how he arrived in his current predicament. That is your obligation under the laws of our organisation.

Advise us of the steps you have taken in this matter.

May the hand of The Great Gargoyle rest lightly on your shoulder and The Dancing Yellow Sprite be forever at your knee.

Brother Walton

Brother Walton
Secretary to the First Knight of the Brazen Serpent

OFFICE OF THE MAYOR

Lambeth Town Hall
Lambeth Walk
Lambeth
London SW2

Terrence Milligan
Governor
Wormwood Scrubs
Du Cane Road
London W12

5 September 1973

Dear Terry

How are Jane and the kids? It is a long time since we last saw you at the Mayor's Banquet. What a night that turned out to be. Remember the roast boar? I ended up £50 to the good after betting against the room that you could eat the whole head. People wouldn't have believed that unless they saw it with their own eyes. And those that did mainly wished they hadn't.

The reason for my letter is to ask about one of your 'guests', a certain Mr Boyce. He got himself into a bit of a pickle over a small matter of embezzlement, which I'm sure was actually only a misunderstanding. As was the fraudulent conversion of travellers cheques. And perverting the course of justice. And perjury. And attempting to bribe the Mayor of Lambeth (not me, my predecessor, now also one of your 'guests').

Mr Boyce is well known to myself and a number of my associates and we can testify to his general good character. In fact, one of my associates owns the villa in Alicante where you and June took the kids on holiday last month. It could be made available to you again for another family holiday, or perhaps a short break with your young secretary who accompanied you on your fact-finding mission to Amsterdam, where another of my associates enjoyed dinner with you both at the Hole In The Dyke club. Superb entertainment from the dancers there, I am told.

You will see what you can do for our Mr Boyce, won't you?

Love to Jane.

best wishes

Alan Stanhope

Mayor Alan Stanhope

BOYCIE ALWAYS DID HAVE
A TRICK UP HIS SLEEVE!

Dear Boycie

Sorry if the note is a bit crumpled. An associate of ours smuggled it out of the visitors' room and had to fold it up very small to hide it where he did.

Hope you are well, fit and healthy, because that way Tony can do so much more damage when I let him off his leash. He's just itching to get at you and when he has an itch, he likes to scratch it with a baseball bat or a crow bar.

You see, we know it was you what grassed us up to the Old Bill.

You might think that you are safe with us on the inside and you out there free as a bird. But you are reading this note, right? And that means that we can reach you. Our brief reckons that he'll have us out on parole in no time – and that's when your time is up.

No one snitches on the Driscoll Brothers.

We'll be seeing you soon. Tony is looking forward to it. He's been practising a tasty little uppercut that he plans to land right on your hooter. He started off by punching the furniture in our cell. So far he's knocked the stuffing out of four mattresses, two prison wardens and a police horse.

Give our love to Marlene.
Well, everyone else has, haven't they?

Danny

BOYCIE WITH THE DRISCOLL
BROTHERS IN HAPPIER TIMES!

Winterdown Farm
Oakham, Shropshire

An attractive mixed arable and livestock farm
In all extending to 72.60 hectares (179.40 acres) or thereabouts

Winterdown Farm
A substantial range of farm buildings
Arable 50.65 hectares (125.14 acres) • Pasture 18.73 hectares (46.29 acres)
Woodland 1.88 hectares (4.65 acres)
Farm equipment is available by separate negotiation

Winterdown Farmhouse
The beautiful 18th century farmhouse comprises a substantial two storey
dwelling with additional attic rooms. The property sits adjacent to the
farmstead, with lawned gardens and a paved area extending around 3 sides.

Beautiful views...

...an historical home to enjoy

Excerpts from John Sullivan's personal scripts and notes

1983-1988

ONLY FOOLS & HORSES

"Homesick Blues"

The lawn-mower, on ~~ensure~~ Grandads chair.

Miss Mackenzie calls (1st time). Rod ends up giving her a bollocking. She decides to help. (During all this Del is trying to chat her up. (Offers her a drink - lowers the lights, music etc)
   This scene continues into the "Chelsea game" ~~Grandads~~ gag.

Grandads bedroom scene.

Final scene, Miss Mackenzie calls with the tray to the new bungalow. Del tries to date her (after smacking her arse - "Fancy a curry?"

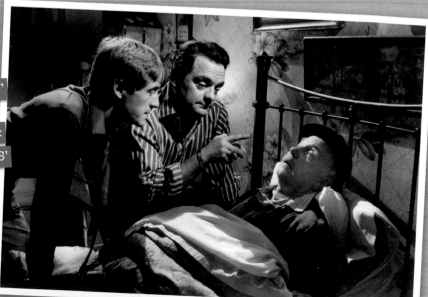

JOHN SULLIVAN WOULD SAVE THE 'FANCY A CURRY' EXCHANGE FOR THE LATER SERIES 3 EPISODE: 'YESTERDAY NEVER COMES'

SCENE. STUDIO

INT. NIGHT. THE TROTTERS LOUNGE

DEL, DRESSED CASUALLY, IS
SCATTERING A FEW OLD SHIRTS
AND DOCKETS ETC AROUND THE LOUNGE.

ROD ENTERS ROOM THROUGH AREA.

ROD:
What are you doing?

DEL:
~~I'm trying to make the place look
untidy and impoverished~~
I'm getting the place ready for
Miss Mackenzie. I want it to
look untidy and impoverished.

ROD:
~~Why~~ So why didn't you just
leave it as it was?

DEL:
Oi, oi, oi! That's enough of that!

ROD:
This sort of thing won't impress
her Del!

DEL:
Look, these old ministers from the
council love a bit of poverty —
it makes 'em feel good.

ROD:

You don't know her Del, she's not
like that!

DEL:

But I know how these old biddies
minds work! — Trust me Rodders,
just trust me will you?
WE HEAR A RING AT BELL.
Go'n, that'll be her.
ROD EXITS TO HALL.

DEL SLUMPS DOWN IN ARMCHAIR.

ROD:

O.K! — (STOPS AT DOOR) Oh clear
the place up a bit Del, it looks
horrible!

DEL:

Just let her in Rodney!

ROD EXITS.

DEL RUFFLES HIS HAIR IN MIRROR.
THEN SLUMPS AT TABLE TRYING
TO GIVE THE IMPRESSION OF SOMEONE
DISTRAUGHT WITH WORRY.
ROD ENTERS.

ROD:

Del, this is Miss Mackenzie!

MISS M ENTERS, SHE IS A 30 YEAR OLD
VERY ATTRACTIVE AND SMARTLY DRESSED
WOMAN.

DEL TRACK. ##

DEL:

(STRAIGHTENING HIS HAIR) Miss Mackenzie, au chanty (KISSES HER HAND)

MISS M:

(TRACK, SHE HAS NEVER BEEN GREETED LIKE THIS BY A TENANT) Oh, thank you Mrs Trotter.

ROD TRACK TO DELS BEHAVIOUR, IT'S ABOUT PAR FOR THE COURSE.

DEL:

Do sit down Miss Mackenzie. (REMOVES A COUPLE OF THE OLD SLEEVES) Clean this place up a bit will you Rodney! (TO MISS M) He leaves it looking like a pig sty!

ROD:

Me?

DEL:

(TO MISS M) Still, his heart's in the right place. — I'm not sure if everything else 'is'. (LAUGHS) Would you like something to drink Miss Mackenzie? Tea, coffee, a pina colada?

MISS M:

MISS M:
Margaret.

DEL:
Oh Margaret, that's my most favourite name. Did you know there's a princess named after you!

MISS M:
Yes, I have heard about her.

DEL:
And a prime minister!

MISS M:
Yes!

DEL
My name's Derek —

MISS M:
Did you know there's a crane named after you!

LOUNGE

THE ROOM IS NOW IN SUBUED LIGHT. (SIDELIGHTS). A ROMANTIC RECORD IS PLAYING ON STEREO.

DEL IS AT DRINKS CABINET PUTTING THE FINAL TOUCHES TO OUR (HIS) COCKTAILS.

MISS M IS FINDING IT DIFFICULT TO WRITE IN THE SEMI-DARK.

DEL BRINGS THE COCKTAIL TO HER.

DEL:
Try that Margarette.

MISS. M:
(REACTS) What is it?

DEL:
It's a Tequila Sunset!

MISS M:
(TAKES A SMALL SIP. REACTS) It tastes like gin!

DEL:
Yeah, I aint got no Tequila!

MISS M:

DEL:
What did you do before you
worked for the council?

MISS M:
I went to school.

DEL:
Oh I see. So you always
wanted to work for the council
did you?

MISS M:
Well not really. I don't think
any ambitious young school leavers
actually set their sights on
"working for the council"? It's
the sort of job one tends to
drift into. No, when I left
school I wanted to be a choreographer

DEL:
Really? — That's funny 'coz I
often thought about joining
the medical proffession as well.

MISS M:
No, a choreographer! I wanted
to teach dance!

DEL:
Oh, that sort of choreographer!
With you now! — I was always
interested in dance meself.

MISS M:
Really? — I went to the London
school of Dance in Chelsea.

DEL:
I went to the Arthur Murray school
in ~~Lewis~~ Deptford.

well, apres moi ~~&~~ le deluge as they say in ~~the~~
Grenobles.

MISS M:
(REACT) Yes! yes, of corse.
Well I'm glad we got that cleared up!

The drums banged out all night long,
sending a message of hope and joy
to the for corners of this mighty estate.
"Bwana Rodney, he come daylight!"

ROD:
You reckon?

DEL:
Oh yes, the moment the news spread
that you'd become chairman of the
tenants association, there was a new
vibrance in the old place! I mean up until
now who have they had to look after
the estate? Basil — bloody 'ell Basil
couldn't keep a rabbit going with lettuce!

Then council wallahs lose respect for you if you don't kick up a fuss! You don't seem to understand the powerful position you're in! When you speak, the town hall trembles.

ROD:
(PASSES RON THROUGH) Yeah!! — I'll phone her now!

DEL:
Good boy, you know it makes sense.

ROD:
~~It's your dream and our nightmare~~
Your dream has become our nightmare.

DEL:
Ooo I like it Rodders.

ROD:
Now I am not willing to stand idley by and watch as our flesh and blood suffer. If I don't get the transfer that I demand I will create a hurricane of social unrest

ONLY FOOLS

"FRIDAY THE 14TH"

SCENE 1. STUDIO
INT. DAY. THE TROTTERS LOUNGE

DEL ENTERS CARRYING THREE FISHING RODS,
KEEP NETS, AND ALL THAT ANGLING PARAPHANALIA.
HE WEARS A FISHERMANS HAT

~~DEL CARRYING THREE FISHING RODS.~~

DEL:
Guess what we're doing the
weekend?
ROD: (EATING A MEAL)
~~We're going golfing!~~ Giss a clue!
DEL:
No Rodney - look at the
clues - fishing (rod) - (OPENS A
TIN AND SHOVES IT IN FRONT OF RODS
FACE) Maggots!,
ROD:
Tonight'! - Do you mind, I'm
eating - or rather was eating, chicken
and rice!

SCENE . FILM
EXT. DAY. A BY-PASS
ROAD
A ⟨ SIGN INDICATES⟩ "THE WEST".
~~THE~~ VAN PASSES US , DEL DRIVING,
ROD IN PASSENGER SEAT.

ROD:
(V.O.) ⟨BEST BING CROSBY⟩ HI
Gone
poaching ~~~~ boba bob - put a
sign up on the door, Sire
poaching —

DEL:
(V.O) ~~YOU~~ You keep on Rodney
and you'll get a smack right
in the ear'ole!

MIX to

★ ONLY FOOLS AND HORSES...★

WRITTEN BY JOHN SULLIVAN
starring DAVID JASON, NICHOLAS LYNDHURST

★ BBC TELEVISION CENTRE ★
SUNDAY 3rd MARCH

DOORS OPEN AT 7.30
DOORS CLOSE AT 8.15pm

CHILDREN UNDER 14
★ NOT ADMITTED ★

COMPLIMENTARY TICKET
★ NOT FOR SALE ★

JOHN SULLIVAN

BBC LIGHT ENTERTAINMENT, TELEVISION   Programme Ident. No:

REHEARSAL SCRIPT   1/LLC F168 D

Production Office: 4128 T.C.
                       576-1558
                       or Ext. 2153

" ONLY   FOOLS   AND   HORSES.... "

by

JOHN   SULLIVAN

Christmas Programme 1983

(3rd Year)

"Thicker Than Water"

Producer/Director .... RAY BUTT
Production Manager .... ANDY SMITH
Production Assistant .... PENNY THOMPSON
A.F.M. .... TONY DOW

Designer .... BRYAN ELLIS
Assistant .... STEVE KEOGH
Costume Designer .... DINAH COLLIN
Make-Up Designer .... DENISE BARON

Properties Buyer .... PENNY ROLLINSON

The sending of this script does not constitute an offer
of a contract for any part therein.

SCENE 3. STUDIO. INT. DAY. THE TROTTERS LOUNGE.

GRANDAD IS CLEARING AWAY CROCKERY FROM TABLE. DEL AND ROD ENTER FROM HALL.

DEL.
Alright Grandad? We've had a good morning! I love this time of year. No sooner have you stopped flogging over-priced christmas bargains, when you start flogging over-priced new year bargains!

GRANDAD.
You finished for the day already?

ROD.
Yeah, we decided to have an early one! I mean the holidays might be over but we're still in the festive spirit ain't we Del?

DEL.
In more ways than one my son! Here, where's the ghost of christma past?

- 24 -

DEL AT MIRROR.
ROD IN OLD CLOTHES READING PAPER.

DEL:
Where's the ghost of christmas past?

GRAN:
He's not here Del!

DEL:
You mean he's gone?

GRAN:
Only ~~down the road for a drink~~ to the New Years Eve do!

DEL:
Oh! I thought it was too good to be true!

GRAN:
You talk about your own father as if he's an alien! You seem to think of him as E.T!

DEL:
No I don't Grandad. E.T. went home! (TO ROD) Oi Weasel, you coming to the New Years do or not?

ROD.
(REACT) Yeah, I'll soon
set changed! Shame
really, there's a film on
tonight about your love
life!

DEL.
Yeah, what is it a
Warren Beatty film?

ROD.
No. 101 Dalmations!,

DEL PICKS UP ENVELOPER.

DEL.
You cheeky little —
what's this?

GRANDAD.
He's not here Del.

DEL.
(HOPEFULLY) You mean he's gone?

GRANDAD.
Only down the road for a drink!

DEL.
Oh!

GRANDAD.
You shouldn't be like that towards
your father Del! You talk about
him as if he was a stranger!

DEL.
Well after eighteen years he's
hardly close is he?

ROD.
I know what Grandad means. You seem
to think of him as an alien. Sort
of, E.T.!

- 25 -

DEL.
I don't think of him like that
Rodney. E.T. went home!

GRANDAD. ~~They~~
~~A couple of letters~~ arrived
~~for you two~~ this morning. I think
it's the results of your tests!

WE SEE THE TWO BROWN ENVELOPES.
DEL AND ROD REACT.
THEY PICK UP THEIR RESPECTIVE
ENVELOPES CAUTIOUSLY.

DEL.
(TO GRANDAD) Oi, these have been
opened!

GRANDAD.
Well that must have bin your Dad.

DEL.
Well the saucy....

GRANDAD.
You can't blame him Del. I suppose
he was too worried to wait for you!

- 26 -

Series 5   50/LLCI 153E

"ONLY FOOLS AND HORSES ...."

EPISODE THREE: "THE LONGEST NIGHT"

STORY ORDER

PAGE	SCENE NO. & DESCRIPTION	CHARACTERS	DAY/NIGHT	NOTES
1	SCENE 1: EXT. DAY. VERY MODERN SUPERSTORE Establishing shot	S/A's?	DAY 1 afternoon	Film
2-3	SCENE 1A: INT. DAY. THE SUPERSTORE The Trotters are at the checkout of the supermarket - buying groceries.	DEL RODNEY ALBERT SHEILA (Checkout girl) S/A's?	DAY 1 afternoon	Film
4-6	SCENE 2 : EXT. DAY. THE SUPERSTORE The Trotters are stopped outside the supermarket by the Security Officer. They follow him inside. Del thinks he's won £1,000 for being millionth customer.	DEL RODNEY ALBERT TOM (Security Officer) S/A's?	DAY 1 afternoon	Film
7-8	SCENE 3: INT. DAY. A SMALL CORRIDOR On the way to the Manager's office - they are arguing about which one of them is the millionth customer.	DEL RODNEY ALBERT TOM	DAY 1 afternoon	Studio
9-17	SCENE 4: INT. DAY. THE MANAGER'S OFFICE The Manager accuses them of shoplifting.	MR. PETERSON (Manager) TOM DEL RODNEY ALBERT	DAY 1 afternoon (approx. 5pm)	Studio
18-20	SCENE 5: INT. DAY. THE SUPERSTORE A black youth, Lennox, is openly shoplifting from the store. He exits from the store loaded with goods.	LENNOX SHEILA TOM WOMAN (Kiosk) (2 lines) Old Lady(no lines) S/A's in Store	DAY 1 early evening 6 p.m.	Film

LENN.
I don't wanna stay here anymore
than you do! But have you any
idea how much is in that safe?
There's about ~~sixty~~ grand!

ROD. (TO MR P)
~~You're kidding~~? That fare?

MR P:
& I'm afraid so.
It's a bank holiday
tomorrow, this is our
busiest day.

LENN.
No cross my heart! It's pay day
tomorrow, so there's all the
wages <u>plus</u> todays takings <u>plus</u>
they're giving a thousand pound
to the millionth customer!

THE TROTTERS LOOK SICK.

ROD.
But these days they pay wages by
cheque!

LENN.
Not here they don't!

DEL.
(TO TOM) Is that right?

- 31 -

TOM.
Yeah. We tried paying 'em by
cheque but the computer kept
messing their wages up.

MR.P.
They threatened strike action
so we had to go back to the old
system.

LENN.
(TAPS HIS TEMPLE WITH GUN. TO DEL)
See, planning! Right, let's all
settle down then. It's only fourteen
hours, it'll soon go.

EVERYONE SITS.

DEL.
(TO ROD) I had a date tonight with
that little croupier bird from the
One Eleven Club. Charming sort. Well
spoken, cordon bleu cook and does the
business! It could be months before I
get another crack at her!

ROD.
Yeah? I'm choked for you!

MIX TO.   - 32 -

SCENE 9. STUDIO. INT. NIGHT. THE
MANAGERS OFFICE.

THE ROOM IS IN DARKNESS EXCEPT
FOR LIGHT FROM WINDOW. EVERYONE
IS SITTING, FEAR HAS BEEN
REPLACED BY BOREDOM.

LENNOX HAS HIS FEET UP ON MISS T'S
DESK.

ROD PRODUCES HIS TIN OF ROLL-UPS.
OPENS IT TO FIND IT IS EMPTY.

ROD.
(QUIETLY TO DEL) ~~I'm out of tobacco.~~

Got any cigars on you?

Anyway, I thought you'd
packed in smoking?

ROD.
well, I have!

DEL.
well this'll help you won't it!

DEL.
No, I smoked me last one about an

hour ago. ~~This'll be a good chance~~
~~for you to give smoking the elbow.~~

ROD.
Oh yeah, a gun at yer head's just

the sort of incentive you need annit!

I'm like a bloke standing in front of

a firing squad and turning down the

offer of a last fag. (POSH ACCENT)

'No thankyou I'm trying to give them

up!'

- 33 -

DEL.
(REFERRING TO LENNOX) He aint
gonna hurt no-one! You don't
believe that guff about him
being a villian and an hard man
do you? He's just a ~~frightened~~
kid tryna get himself a few bob.

I tell you, he's more frightened than us.

ALB.
He's still got a gun though!

DEL.
Yeah, but as long as we don't
panic him he won't use it. I
tell you, he's more frightened
than us!

ROD.
Aah bless him!

DEL SQUINTS INTO THE DARK CORNER
WHERE LENNOX IS.

DEL.
You still there son?

- 34 -

LENN.
Yeah, what d'you want?

DEL.
How about putting a light on,
see what we're about.

LENN.
But passers-by might see the
light!

DEL.
Well pull the blinds then!

LENN.
Oh yeah!...(TO TOM) Okay, I want
you to do exactly as I say.

TOM.
Anything you say, you're the
boss.

LENN.
I want you to switch the light on
then pull the blinds.

DEL.
No no, pull the blinds then switch
the light on!

- 35 -

D: an affair with a married woman

J: (As we know) there is much work to be done. use

ONLY FOOLS AND HORSES...!

By

JOHN SULLIVAN

CHRISTMAS SPECIAL '87

The Frog's Legacy

SCENE 1. STUDIO.

INT. NIGHT. THE NAGS HEAD.

DEL AND ROD ARE AT COUNTER.

ALB IS SEATED AT NEAR-BY TABLE.

TRIGGER IS CHATTING TO ALB.

DEL:

(CALLS) Michael - Mike.

MIKE:

(BORED WITH DELS EFFORTS TO SELL HIM SOMETHING - ANYTHING) What is it now?

DEL:

This is your lucky night. (PRODUCES A COLOUR BROCHURE OF A COMPUTER. "THE RAJAH 1200")

DEL CONT'D.

DEL CONT'D.

What about that for a home computer eh, Mike?
It's got 64K, U.H.F Output, a megabite
disc-drive, It's got ROM it's got RAM,
it's got em, red and green lights, everything!

MIKE:
What do I want with a computer?

DEL:
What does he want with a computer?
Everyone's got a computer these days!

MIKE:
Have you got one?

ROD:
He's got twenty five!

DEL:
Yes, thankyou, Rodney! Michael, this
particular model retails at three hundred
and ninety nine pounds of the realm.
I'm giving it to you for one hundred and
fifty, I'll even chuck a joy stick in.
See, you can process all your data.

MIKE:
And what exactly does that mean?

DEL:
Well it means you can... you can... tell
him what it means, Rodney.(TO MIKE)
He's taken a course in this, he came
top of his class.

-2-

THE SENDING OF THIS SCRIPT DOES NOT CONSTITUTE AN OFFER OF A CONTRACT FOR ANY PART IN IT.

BBC TELEVISION

LIGHT ENTERTAINMENT (COMEDY) REHEARSAL SCRIPT

"ONLY FOOLS AND HORSES" Series 'F'

by

JOHN SULLIVAN

"Dates"

Episode 1.

Producer .... GARETH GWENLAN
Director .... TONY DOW
Production Manager .... ADRIAN PEGG
Production Assistant .... AMITA LOCHAB
Assistant Floor Manager .... KERRY WADDELL

* *

Programme No: 1/LLC K751X

Production Office: Room 7022 TV Centre
Tel. 01-743-8000 Ext. 2153/1558
DL: 01-576-1558

* *

Filming: 7th November-2nd December 1988

Studio Recording: Saturday 10th & Sunday 11th December 1988

TX DATE: SUNDAY 25TH DECEMBER 1988

```
'ONLY FOOLS AND HORSES' CAST LIST          EPISODE 1.

   DEL ..................... DAVID JASON          (Film/Studio)

   RODNEY ................. NICHOLAS LYNDHURST     (Film/Studio)

   ALBERT ................. BUSTER MERRYFIELD      (Studio only)

   BOYCIE ................                         (Studio only)

   TRIGGER ...............                         (Film/Studio)

   MARLENE ...............                         (Studio only)

   RAQUEL . ..............                         (Film/Studio)

   MICKY .................                         (Studio only)

   JEVON .................                         (Studio only)

   CHRIS .................                         (Studio only)

   NERYS .................                         (Film/Studio)

   DATADATE AGENT ........                         (Studio only)

   SONIA .................                         (Film only)

   CHARLES ...............                         (Film only)

   P.C. ..................                         (Film/Studio)

   W.P.C. ................                         (Film/Studio)

   SID ...................                         (Studio only)

   NAVAL OFFICER .........                         (Studio only)

   MRS. SANSOM ...........                         (Studio only - OOV)
```

Non-Speaking Artists:

```
People in Nags Head pub
Yobs in car
People in streets during car chase
Car driver in chase
Waiter in Italian restaurant
Woman in Italian restaurant
Customers in Italian restaurant
People outside Datadate Agency
Police at Victoria Station
People at Victoria Station
Customers in Savoy restaurant
Market Cafe customers
```

Episode 1   'ONLY FOOLS AND HORSES'

PAGES	SCENE/DESCRIPTION	CHARACTERS	CAM/SOUND	SHOTS
	OPENING TITLES			
1-13	1. INT. TROTTERS' LOUNGE. STUDIO. (Day 1 - Morning) Albert reminds the boys about his birthday	DEL RODNEY ALBERT		
14-29	2. INT. NAG'S HEAD PUB. STUDIO (Day 1 - Lunchtime) Trigger's got a date; Boycie tells Del about the Lodge; Del arranges a party for Albert	ALBERT MIKE BOYCIE TRIGGER DEL RODNEY MICKY JEVON Extras		
30	3. EXT. ITALIAN RESTAURANT. STUDIO. (Day 1 - Lunchtime) Del sees Trigger with the date in the restaurant	DEL TRIGGER Waiter Woman Extras		
31-38	4. INT. NAG'S HEAD PUB. STUDIO. (Day 1 - Lunchtime) Rodney makes a date with Nerys	RODNEY MICKY JEVON NERYS CHRIS MIKE BOYCIE Extras		

Episode 1   'ONLY FOOLS AND HORSES'

PAGES	SCENE/DESCRIPTION	CHARACTERS	CAM/SOUND	SHOTS
39	5. EXT. BUSY LONDON STREET. FILM. (Day 1 - Lunchtime) The van is parked outside the Datadate Agency	Extras		
40-49	6. INT. DATADATE AGENCY. STUDIO. (Day 1 - Lunchtime) Del gets fixed up with a date	DEL AGENT		
50-61	7. INT. TROTTERS LOUNGE. STUDIO. (Day 2 - Lunchtime) A week later - Del and Rodney are going on their dates	DEL RODNEY ALBERT		
62	8. EXT. VICTORIA STATION. FILM. (Day 2 - 12.30pm)	DEL Policeman Extras		

SCENE SIX. INT. DATADATE AGENCY.

DAY. STUDIO.

IT IS A LIGHT AND
PLEASANT MODERN OFFICE.

THE AGENT IS A SMARTLY-
DRESSED MAN IN HIS MID-
THIRTIES. HE HAS A
COMPUTER AND SCREEN IN
FRONT OF HIM INTO WHICH
HE PRINTS INFORMATION
FROM DEL'S ANSWERS.

AGENT:
So can you tell me, what kind of

person are you looking for?

DEL:
Well ... a bird.

AGENT:
Yes. But are there are

particular requirements?

DEL:
A local bird if possible, I don't

want too much of that driving

lark.

40

IN THE FINAL EPISODE, THE DATING AGENCY WAS CHANGED FROM 'DATADATE' TO 'TECHNOMATCH'

AGENT:
(HITS A FEW KEYS) So you're not looking for a special <u>type</u> of person?

DEL:
Well she's gotta be a bit of a sort!

AGENT:
A bit of a sort?

DEL:
Well, everything in the right place, you know. She must be a bit refined.

AGENT:
Must she! (KEYS THIS IN)

DEL:
Oh yes. I don't want you lumbering me with some old bow-wow who don't know a Liebfraumilk from a can of Tizer!

THE AGENTS EXPRESSION
TELLS US THAT HE HAS
NEVER MET ANYONE LIKE
DEL BEFORE.

41

AGENT:
Quite!

DEL:
I'm a bit of a culture vulture

meself you see.

AGENT:
Ah, a man of the arts.

DEL:
Oh yes, you can't whack it. And

you can tell the lucky lady that

she is guaranteed a steak meal.

AGENT:
(FAZED) A steak meal?

DEL:
Guaranteed! You wanna put that

on yer floppy disc?

AGENT:
What? Yes, I'll make a note.

(KEYS IN) A steak meal. Now

please don't feel pressurised by

this next question. We're not

trying to force you into any

decision or commitment. The

question is asked simply to

protect our clients.

42

SCENE EIGHT. EXT. VICTORIA

STATION. DAY. FILM.

WE SEE DEL (IN HIS CAMEL
HAIR COAT) AND THE BOUQUET
WAITING BENEATH THE CLOCK
IN THE MAIN CONCOURSE OF
THE STATION.

HE PACES A SMALL AREA
NERVOUSLY.

HE CHECKS THE CLOCK WHICH
STANDS AT 12.30. HE CHECKS
THIS AGAINST HIS WATCH. NOW
RECHECKS HIS WATCH AND TAPS
IT A FEW TIMES AS IF IT HAS
GONE WRONG.

WE SEE A POLICEMAN PATROLLING
THE STATION. HE OBSERVES DEL
(NOT SUSPICIOUSLY AT THIS
POINT) MORE OUT OF INTEREST,
HE'S NEVER SEEN SUCH A LARGE
BOUQUET.

DEL SMILES NERVOUSLY TO THE
POLICEMAN.

BY THE TIME 'DATES' REACHED TV SCREENS
VICTORIA STATION WAS CHANGED TO WATERLOO

62

MARLENE
★ ★ ★ ★ ★ ★ ★ ★ ★

ALL THE BOYS
REMEMBER MARLENE!

Dockside Secondary Modern School
Peckham, London SE15

16 May 1963
Mr and Mrs Lane
17 Falmouth Street
Peckham
London SE15

Dear Mr and Mrs Lane

I am writing to you to inform you that Marlene was sent home from school today after her seventh warning about her attire.

At Dockside Secondary Modern we do have rules about school uniform but Marlene does not interpret those rules in anything approaching the same way as any of the other girls, apart, perhaps, from the girls whose uniforms Marlene has been 'modernising' in the domestic education block.

Shoes should have sensible heels suitable for walking. Marlene's shoes have heels so high and thin that she has twice found herself unable to move, her heels having bored into the classroom floorboards.

I am not averse to the uniform following fashion trends to a degree, but the rules state quite clearly that girls' skirts should be no more than two inches above the knee. Marlene's is not a short skirt, it's more of a thick belt.

We also have an issue with the tattoo of a heart with a dagger through it on Marlene's thigh – which we should never, in any case, be able to see. Imagine my surprise when I discovered that you, Mr Lane, had drawn the tattoo. It may be your profession but it is surely not acceptable to practice on your own daughter!

The uniform blouse is, of course, white. At no time has the school uniform committee ever considered adopting a leopardskin print design, yet Marlene seems to think this is acceptable.

Marlene's passion for fashion is only equalled by her enthusiasm for attracting the attention of the older boys, most of the male teachers, passing lorry drivers, the fathers of other pupils and even Percy, the school caretaker, who is due to retire next month!

Marlene should take the next two days to consider how she might change her attitude to the school and the way she presents herself when she returns to school.

Yours sincerely

T Moore

Miss 'T' Moore
Deputy Head (Girls)

PADDY O'BRIAN
Turf Accountant

17 Lewisham Grove, Lewisham, London SE12

Letter of Reference

To Whom It May Concern,

Marlene Lane has worked in my Bookies Office in Lewisham for nearly three years, so she has. She may not always have turned up for work exactly on time but it was always a pleasure to hear her motorbike come roaring down the Grove.

In her time with us, my regulars came to know Marlene (some a lot better than others) as Shaunessy's Little Angel. She was only supposed to be doing the odd bit of filing, tidying up, running errands and making the tea but, to be sure, the daily take went up by at least a third when Marlene was working. She's a cracking lass. She had a way with her, so she did. With just a wee wink of the eye or a wiggle of the hips she had them filling out betting slips like there was no tomorrow.

Marlene always dressed beautifully, in right good taste and modern with it. There must have been a fair old draft whistling up those short skirts when she rode along on that motorbike and there was always a book running in the shop about when she would next bend over to pick something up off the floor.

It always raised a few eyebrows when I said she's a great craic, so suffice to say that she has a bubbly personality, the gift of the gab and can charm the birds out of the trees.

Marlene would be a definite asset to any business where your main customers are men, so she would.

Yours sincerely

Paddy O'Brian

Paddy O'Brian

MARLENE -
ALWAYS ONE OF THE
CLASSIEST BIRDS
IN THE PARISH

Marlene adored her great dane – Duke!

Marlene and Boycie have their hairy moments...

...but they still make time for regular anniversary dos!

BSA MOTORCYCLES
British Small Arms Company, Armoury Way, Birmingham

BSA
THE MOST POPULAR MOTOR CYCLE IN THE WORLD

Miss Marlene Lane
17 Falmouth Street
Peckham
London SE15

12 October 1964

Re: Vibration on BSA D7 Bantam Super

Dear Miss Lane

Thank you for your letter regarding your Bantam Super.
At first we were a little concerned about your vivid
description of the engine vibrations coming up through the
saddle. While all motorcycles cause a degree of vibration,
the D7 is regarded as having a smooth-running motor and we
have never had any complaints about excessive vibration
before, even when the unit is running at the maximum
recommended revolutions.

Then we realised that what you were actually asking was
how you might INCREASE the vibration. I am afraid that is
something upon which we cannot advise.

I hope that your BSA motorcycle continues to provide you
with pleasurable transport for many years to come and that
you continue to enjoy riding to the full.

Yours sincerely

William Jones

William Jones
Customer Services Manager

THEIR MOST RECENT PARTY
WAS FOR THEIR RUBY
ANNIVERSARY IN 2009!

Dear Del

I guess you heard that me and Boycie got engaged. I saw you looking across at me in the Nag's Head and you looked ever so sad. Don't be sad, Del. That's not the Del Boy everyone knows and loves.

We had some good times together, didn't we? Remember that time we went dancing up the Alexandra Palace and kept on dancing in the park until the sun came up? We had a lot of fun, Del, but we were always too alike, you and me. We liked all the same things and we would have ended up getting right on each other's wick, and fallin out and fightin ... and I couldn't bear that.

I want us always to be friends, but I've decided that my future is with Boycie. He treats me well enough, he ain't such a bad sort and he ain't short of a bob or two. I think I need that sort of security in my life, Del.

Next time we see each other, give's a smile. You'll always be special to me, and we'll always have Ally Pally.

love Marlene

Me and Marlene often still have a special moment...

...or two!

THE BROMPTON FERTILITY CLINIC

Brompton Fertility Clinic, Brompton Road, London SW4

21 August 1986

Dear Mr and Mrs Boyce

Further to the recent tests you undertook here at the clinic, we can confirm that there is an abnormality with Mr Boyce's sperm count.

In fact, the count is not as far below normal as we would expect, but the sperms themselves are not performing as well as we might hope. In layman's terms, they appear to be a little disinterested. While we would expect to see them swimming around energetically, they appear instead to be rather lethargic. They just can't be bothered.

We would recommend that Mr Boyce cut back on the cognac and cigars for a few weeks before you arrange for another test. That way the little devils might regain some of their vitality and start swimming like Olympic champions - not that you would really want them wriggling around in a swimming pool, of course.

Yours sincerely

Dr W Allen

Dr W Allen

MARLENE WAS ALWAYS DEVASTATED ABOUT NOT HAVING A LITTLE CHAVY...

It's a BOY

Congratulations, Marlene!

We ain't seen each other since I left the Nag's Head to go work in the Tinkerbell Club in Soho. I been promoted from the Entertainment Floor to Office Administrator now, mainly on account of how I kept breaking me pole, but one of our punters said that you finally got knocked up.

Who'd have thought it, eh? Boycie was usually all mouth and no trousers. So I heard. And Del always used to say Boycie was a jaffa. Still, it's lovely that it's worked out for you.

It is his, ain't it? Only kidding! Ha-ha!

love

Joyce

MARLENE'S LITTLE BABY SAILER BOY!

The proud Boyce family at Damien's christening

A mum at last! Marlene in 1989

TYLER IN HIS LATE TEENS

Croydon Cosmetic Procedures
126-128 Purley Rise, Croydon CR15

Mrs Marlene Boyce
17 Kings Avenue
Peckham
London SE15

15 October 2003

Dear Mrs Boyce

Further to your consultation at the surgery I am pleased to confirm that we can book you in for the procedure you have requested on 7 November.

A leaflet explaining what you should bring with you on the day is enclosed. We would like to see you here at 10.00 am on the morning of the appointment. Please do not eat or drink anything 8 hours prior to this time. I would ask you to remember that I am a little nervous around dogs and that our anaesthetist, Mr Karmerkar has a strong allergy to dog hair, so please leave Duke at home this time. Mr Karmerkar's rash is responding to treatment and he hopes to be back at work in time for your procedure.

As we discussed, we are able to enhance your breasts in a number of ways but we would recommend that the augmentation is kept proportionate to your figure. You have a slim frame and we would not be able to achieve the natural appearance that will best suit your build if we were to make the increase in size too dramatic, even if, as your husband said, he 'would want a right couple of whoppers for that price.'

The cost of the surgery is not inconsiderable but it reflects the quality and safety of the work we undertake here. You can be confident, for example, that the silicone implants that we use will not balloon out if you go on a long-haul aircraft flight. Neither will you find them slipping round into your armpits when you are lying on the beach or baking solid in the sunshine. We would not, however, recommend bungee jumping as this has resulted in previous clients giving themselves two black eyes.

If you have any questions about the surgery prior to the above date, then please do get in touch.

Yours sincerely

Dr Sangit Patel

Dr Sangit Patel

for all your post-surgery needs, sho

Marlene had vanished, and Boycie was acting strange...

...but it turned out she was having surgery!

HAMPSHIRE Herald

15p

22 September 1986

BIRD MAN DISAPPEARS

A hang glider pilot who took off from Sundown Hill yesterday has been reported missing.

The man was taking part in a flying session organised by a reputable local organisation, the South Downs Flyers, when he soared off into a cloud.

"We were amazed at the height he achieved," said the Flyers club secretary Andy Williams. "It was his first time with us, but he was an experienced hang glider.

"He was joking before he set off. When I told him that we had good thermals today, he said he was fine in his Y-fronts."

Shortly after taking off, the pilot did hit a thermal - a rising column of air - and gained height rapidly.

"He sounded like he was really enjoying himself," said Mr Williams. "We could hear him roaring and laughing hysterically. The last we saw of him he was heading towards the Isle of Wight and vanished into a cloud."

When they lost track of him, the club called the emergency services and the police were able to piece together part of the bizarre flight from witness statements.

"Officers on the ground interviewed walkers and picnickers in the area," said Sergeant James Turnbull of Hampshire Constabulary. "They reported hearing whooping and shrieking and garbled cries in a cockney accent. One witness claims to have seen a hang glider pilot wearing a heavy woollen coat and loafers, apparently performing mid-air stunts, including a loop-the-loop, but he may have been drunk or just not the full deck."

Profesional set-up...
The South Down Flyers

The pilot never returned to Sundown Hill and his associates there gave up waiting when it got dark.

"We are certain that this individual is no longer on our patch," said Sergeant Turnbull, "as we have unconfirmed reports about where he might have ended up."

Concerned:
Club secretary Andy Williams

Last known course of missing glider

HAMPSHIRE HERALD SPORT – Starts on page 43 – New signing for the Hampshire Blues? // Barker to return?

Andy and Lisa swallowed my stories of being a paratrooper!

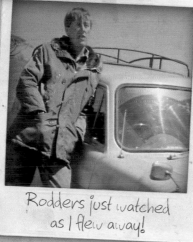

Rodders just watched as I flew away!

THEY DO THIS FOR FUN?
I WAS SO GLAD TO GET BACK
TO THE TERRA-COTTA!

SURREY GAZETTE

22 September 1986

TV BLACKOUT AT REDHILL

Viewers in the Redhill area lost television reception last night following an incident at the local transmission mast.

Transmissions went off-air after the mast sustained damage when a hang glider crashed into it. A local couple were parked in a quiet spot near the mast when the crash happened.

"We were just sitting there minding our own business, like," said Mr James Milton, "and enjoying the sunset. Then there was a bang and a flash high above us and this bloke came crashing in through the sunroof!"

Mr Milton and his fiancee, Emma, were driven straight to Redhill Hospital where they were treated for minor bruises and shock and the hang glider pilot was extricated from the sunroof of their Ford Sierra.

All three were later released from the hospital after being interviewed by officers from Surrey Police.

Peckham *Echo*

12 September 1986 • 18p

CRYING HOLY STATUE MIRACLE IN PECKHAM

People have been flocking to St Mary's Church in Peckham to witness what many believe to be a genuine miracle as a statue of the Virgin Mary weeps real tears.

PARISH PRIEST FATHER O'KEITH first noticed the phenomenon after taking confession from a parishioner and word about what is being called The Peckham Miracle quickly spread.

"I couldn't believe my eyes when I first saw it," said Father O'Keith. "I looked up and there was the blessed virgin with tears as big as pearls rolling down her cheeks. In my heart I know that she is crying over the plight of the sick and elderly at St Mary's Hospice."

St Mary's Hospice has acted as a refuge and a place where those suffering from terminal illnesses can spend the end of their days in peace and tranquility. The hospice is currently scheduled to be demolished and the elderly locals living there will be sent to other facilities far and wide across London.

"The hospice is a place of great dignity," said Father O'Keith, "but this oasis of calm cannot survive without cash for repairs to the building."

Since the discovery of the weeping statue, Father O'Keith has had local businessman Derek Trotter helping with fund raising for the hospice.

"I truly could not believe me own minces when I saw them tears on the old virgin," said Mr Trotter. "I happened to be in the church when Father O'Keith called to me and I walked meekly to the altar like an artificial lamb. Seeing Mary crying buckets made me well up an all."

Mr Trotter has been co-ordinating fund-raising for the hospice with promoting The Miracle of Peckham.

"If, like me, that veil of tears shed by Holy Mary lifts a veil from your own eyes and gives you renewed faith," said Mr Trotter, "then you've got to come and have a butcher's at this. She don't cry constantly but, like most birds, you can expect it sooner rather than later. Ticket prices are extremely reasonable and you can re-use your ticket stub for one more visit if you don't see no tears. We ain't had any disappointed punters so far and we're well on the way to hitting our target to save the hospice."

Repairs to St Mary's Hospice were estimated at £250,000 with a shortfall of almost £185,000 which Mr Trotter believes they can match through sales of tickets and merchandise.

"Well, you would want a little memento of such a spectacular event, wouldn't you?" he said. "And what better than a genuine 100% natural imitation stone statue of the Virgin Mary that plays *Away In A Manger* and cries real tears? Just lift her arm and she squeezes one out. Only £9.99 - now I can't say fairer than that, can I?"

Father O'Keith   Derek Trotter

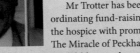

SPORT: Peckham UTD's new stadium opens its turnstiles for the very first time, but can it reverse the fortunes for this difficult season?

PECKHAM ECHO   26 September 1986

NO MORE TEARS FOR PECKHAM MIRACLE

The weeping statue of The Virgin Mary at St Mary's Church in Peckham has stopped crying the tears that created The Peckham Miracle.

"I DON'T KNOW WHAT'S HAPPENED," said parish priest Father O'Keith. "One day she was in floods of tears but for the past few days she hasn't had even a sniffle."

Devotees who crowded into the church to witness the miracle are no longer queueing round the block to gain entry, as they were only a week ago. Some believe that the unusually dry and warm spell of weather we have been enjoying over the past few days may be to blame for the Virgin's tears drying up.

Local businessman, Derek Trotter, who managed the promotional activity surrounding the miracle, dismisses claims that outside influences have led to the end of the tears.

"Some are saying that it was all down to atmosterics," said Mr Trotter, "but the Lord moves in mysterious ways, don't he? The tears were a sign that we had to get up off our arses and do something about the hospice. And we have done, haven't we?"

Not only was enough money raised to save the hospice, but there was also enough to carry out repairs to the church roof, which had been letting in water during periods of heavy rain. Some have been quick to point out that the roof repairs and the lack of tears might be connected.

"Well of course they're connected," said Mr Trotter. "Now that the hospice has been saved and the roof has been repaired, Mary is happy, so she ain't got nothing to cry about has she? And you can't make a woman turn on the water works just because you want her to. It is, at the end of the day, 'Fabrique Belgique,' as the Romans say".

We did it – we saved the Hospice!

ALWAYS UP FOR DOING MY BIT FOR THE MAN ABOVE!

TITCO LOSS LEADERS
★ ★ ★ ★ ★ ★ ★ ★ ★ ★ ★ ★ ★ ★ ★ ★ ★ ★

Report on Underperforming Sales Lines

Rodney C Trotter (DIC)

What the hell was Del thinking about when he bought in some of this stuff?
You'd have to be blind, or stupid or both to fall for any of his sales spiel
when he was flogging this lot. It's not cheap and tacky -
it's not that good. It's utter crap. And this is just the tip of the iceberg.
I've never actually seen what's lurking up the back of the lock-up!

Despite Del's misgivings
I kept TITco sales records

The Rajah 1200 Portable Computer

This computer was about as portable as
the pyramids. It weighed a ton but Del said
that's because it was loaded with technology
and solid state-of-the-art macro chips. It
might as well have been loaded with fish
n chips. And where would you expect a
machine like this to be built? Japan? China?
Germany? None of that. These came straight
from the bristling hub of the hi-tech industry
- Mauritius. A notice in all the papers from
Trading Standards warning that they could
go up in smoke made even Del feel
a bit guilty about
offloading one on
a vicar in Hampshire.

The Olde English Briefcase

Okay, so these looked good at first
glance. At first glance they looked like
leather. They wasn't, but they was the
finest quality Olde English vinyl-covered
cardboard with high-security combination
locks. You had to admire them. You had
to admire them because that's all you
could do with them - the combinations were
locked inside. We ended up dumping all
two dozen of them. Mind you, what
can you expect when you buy dodgy
goods from Trigger?

·R·A·J·A·H·
COMPUTERS

MADE IN MAURITIUS

The Futafax Machine

It were billed as 'The Fax Machine of Tomorrow Today'. Maybe it was ahead of its time. Maybe it delivered faxes to a far off future world. It certainly never sent or received nothing that made any sense to any present-day human. Some interesting flashing lights and whirring noises, but that's about all these things had going for them. Del only sold one and that was to Mike in the Nag's Head. We then got a fax from him that read 'This bl.@£%*$$ machine is tot@$$&&! shi****'. He weren't none too pleased with it.

Lullaby Dolls

Lifelike (not), charming (really not) and loveable (absolutely not) these dolls could do everything a real baby could do - including keep you awake at night! Nobody could ever get a bit of shut-eye with one of these monsters sitting in the corner of the room. They had mad, staring eyes and they was supposed to sing a soothing lullaby at bedtime - but it turned out they only sang in Chinese! It was like listening to Orville singing a take-away menu!

Louvre Doors

Well, there was nothing wrong with these doors. They was good quality. They even stood up to being dropped a few times when they was being lobbed out the warehouse window when I went to pick them up. Trouble was, Del planned to flog them to the builder Brendan O'Shaughnessy who was doing up some houses on an estate, but his contract was cancelled and we were landed with the doors. Since we'd borrowed cash to buy the doors, we were also left owing two grand to Denzil, whose brothers were after our blood.

Crowning Glory Wigs

These were a real bargain. They were only slightly flawed in manufacture, but there was a major flaw when it came to selling the things. Del had plenty of customers lined up and had done a lot of leg work to get a whole bunch of old dears excited about these fantastic wigs. Trouble is, they turned out to be blokes' wigs! All the little old ladies who dreamed of looking like Doris Day would have ended up looking like Rock Hudson instead!

CROWNING GLORY
WIGS OF DISTINCTION

MICKEY PEARCE
★ ★ ★ ★ ★ ★ ★ ★ ★ ★ ★ ★

FASHIONS CAME AND WENT, BUT MICKEY ALWAYS STAYED TRUE TO HIS TRILBY HAT IMAGE!

The Headmaster
Dockside Junior School
Coal Wharf Road
Peckham
London SE15

12 May 1971

Mrs Kathleen Pearce
113 Vasco Da Gama Building
Zanzibar Road
Nyerere Estate
Peckham
London SE15

Dear Mrs Pearce

Your son, Michael, has been attending school regularly over the
past term. He is usually here on Tuesdays and Thursdays. Quite what
he does or where he goes on Mondays, Wednesdays and Fridays I have
no idea. Do you?

When Michael does appear, he insists on wearing an unsightly black
hat with a white or chequered hatband. It is neither stylish
nor attractive and is certainly not part of the approved school
uniform. Michael has only ever been seen to take the hat off once.
He even insisted on wearing it on the rare occasions when he failed
to avoid PE . . . and during lessons at the local swimming baths.
The only time he took off his hat was during an arithmetic test
when the teacher noticed that he had his 'times tables' written
inside the brim.

I would like you to bring Michael to school on Monday morning next
week when I will expect you both in my office at 10.00 am. We can
then discuss with Michael the importance of him attending school
five days a week instead of his usual two.

For the sake of his education I am even prepared to negotiate
terms. If he shows up for school, he can carry on wearing the hat.

Yours sincerely

G S Anderson

G S Anderson
Headmaster

Can you smell that Mickey?
Sheep? Cow? No, its Bull shit!

BEHAVING LIKE A CHILD
COMES NATURALLY TO MICKEY!

185

HIDE 'N' CHIC

Leather Sofas of Distinction

147-151 Station Road, Peckham Trading Estate
Peckham, London SE15

12 August 1977

Mr M Pearce
113 Vasco Da Gama Building
Zanzibar Road
Nyerere Estate
Peckham
London SE15

Dear Mickey

When you walked into my office to pick up your wages
last Thursday, I thought the leather tie you was
wearing looked familiar. Then I spotted where you cut a
strip out the back of our top-of-the-range four-seater.

You ever show your face around here again I'll cut
a strip off you!

You're sacked!

Richard Trimble

Richard Trimble
Manager

A PHOTO TAKEN DURING RODNEY AND MICKY PEARCE'S ILL-FATED JOINT BUSINESS VENTURE!

The moment the young traders knew they were lumbered!

BENIDORM (España)

Wotcher again, Rodders!

Listen, mate, I'm really broken up about what I done, runnin off with our company dosh and all that. I'll make it up to you when we get back and we can carry on makin a mint.

Still roastin hot out here but the sangria is coolin me down!

See ya.

Mickey

Rodney Trotter
Flat 127
Nelson Mandela House
New World Estate
Peckham
London SE15

Mickey Pearce was never the best wingman!

How's it hangin, Rodders?

Hope you got the other two cards what I sent. You'd love it out here, mate, it's all booze, birds, beaches and clubbing. It ain't as cheap as you might think, though. Money's all done. I'm brassic. To cap it all, some tosser nicked me hat while I was asleep on the beach.

Couldn't send me out a few quid till I get back, could ya? Otherwise I'm in dead lumber.

Your best mate,

Mickey

Rodney Trotter
Flat 127
Nelson Mandela House
New World Estate
Peckham
London SE15

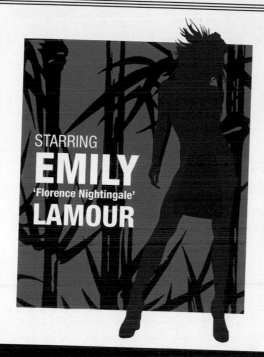

PEARCE MEDIA PRODUCTIONS
Presents

NIGHT NURSE +

She's on **red-hot** duty every night!

DIRECTED BY MICKEY PEARCE

STARRING
EMILY
'Florence Nightingale'
LAMOUR

COMING SOON!
Night Nurse II – The Lady With the Gimp

All the gang were upstairs in the Nags Head to watch...

The leading lady was a hit with the audiance...

But Rodney's surprise cameo did not go down well!

THE WORLD PREMIERE OF NIGHT NURSE WAS
REMEMBERD FOR ALL THE WRONG REASONS!

THE PECKHAM POUNCER

Diary of An Innocent Man - Day 1

It's a safe place, this tank room. Right at the top of the building. They'll never find me here. Not sure how long I've been up here, though. Has it been days? Has it been weeks? Or has it been since just after lunch? Lunch. Wish I hadn't thought of that. Getting hungry again now, ain't I? Best make a list of provisions - I might have to put meself on short rations if I'm to be here a while.

Baked beans	x 4 tins
Corned beef	x 2 tins
Tomato soup	x 3 tins
Spaghetti	x 2 tins
Pineapple chunks	x 1 tin

Shame I forgot the tin opener. Still, a man on the run from the law can't just pop back to his flat for a tin opener, can he? Del says they're calling me The Peckham Pouncer. He says there are mobs roaming the streets ready to string me up from the nearest lamp post - and not by me neck, neither! I wish I had never clapped eyes on that little old lady now. All I did was try to help her when she nearly fell over and she started screaming 'RAPE!' Maybe I shouldn't have said I was a doctor. I only said it to make her shut up. Don't look good though, does it?

Diary of An Innocent Man - Still Day 1 (or is it?)

I must have dozed off for a bit. It is light outside, but does that mean it is still today, or did I sleep all night and it's now tomorrow? Or did I sleep all night and all day and now it's the day after tomorrow? Or maybe I've slept for a thousand years and the world is now run by a race of super-cockroaches that all drive around in little yellow three-wheeled vans searching for the fake doctor that fondles old ladies! There's a window - I can see out. Yes! There they are! Thousands of cockroaches all driving little . . . no . . . hang on a second, Rodders, you're still asleep, ain't ya?

That's better. Awake now. Still no idea what day it is, though. I would check my watch but it's one of them electronic gizmos and you have to press a button to bring up the date. Given that it's a Del Trotter electronic gizmo, it's just as likely to play the Lithuanian national anthem at full volume and that would give me away. Feeling really peckish now though - Peckish of Peckham. Sounds daft, but it's still better than The Peckham Pouncer.

How could anyone think I would grab a granny? I'M INNOCENT!!!!!!!!

Rodders - always up for helping a damsel...

...but blossom is a fruit cake!

Diary of An Innocent Man - Day 2
(or at least the day after yesterday)

Now I know it's another day. When I woke up I could hear Herbie the milkman's milk float and the birds making a right old racket. Still don't know how long I've been up here, though. If only I had thought to scratch a line on the wall like The Bird Man of Alcatraz, or The Prisoner of Zenda or The Man in the Iron Mask, or Ronnie Barker in Porridge. Mind you, the wall in here is metal, so scratching it would make that horrible screechy noise, like someone dragging their fingernails down a blackboard. Jamie Paterson used to do that when we was in primary school. Whenever the teacher went out of the class he would nip up to the blackboard and scrape his fingernails down it. It was guaranteed to upset two kids at the front so much that they wet themselves. Ooooh - I do wish I hadn't thought of that - I'm bustin for a wee now!

I need to concentrate on how I can clear my name. How am I gonna tell the world that I didn't do nothing to that little old lady? I can't very well do that from in here. I need to get out there and try to prove I'm innocent, like Robert Powell in The 39 Steps. Trouble is, Robert Powell only had some murdering spies after him - not a Peckham Posse ready to wrap a noose around his knackers! I'm innocent!

Diary of An Innocent Man
Still Day 2 (but seems like a week)

It's boring in here. I never brought nothing to read. I've read all of the ingredients on the beans, tomato soup and spaghetti. I'm saving the corned beef and pineapple chunks for tomorrow. There's a lot of reading on those labels and by a process of elimination, I think I have worked out all me favourite E numbers. And the spaghetti is well past its sell-by date. Maybe it's just as well. I ain't got no tin opener. I could have died of food poisoning up here and no one would have known. And if they ever did find me, would anyone really care? PECKHAM POUNCER PERVERT POISONED is what they would put in the Peckham Echo.

God it's boring up here. I can't make any noise in case someone hears me. I can't move about, can't whistle, can't sing, can't bear it! I'm getting so as I think I can hear me beard growing. I thought I could feel me toenails growing earlier but it was just a mouse tap dancing on me shoe. I've counted me teeth (30) and the number of teeth in the zip on me trousers (62). Ain't it something when you've got less teeth in your mouth than you do in your trousers?

Hang on a minute. Someone's coming. It's Del! It's me brother! He's found me! Wait, though. Calm down Rodders. Act cool. You didn't want to be found, remember? I hope he's brought a tin opener.

DEL WORKED OUT WHERE TO FIND ME

Life in hiding is not easy... especially with no tin opener!

DENZIL
★ ★ ★ ★ ★ ★ ★ ★

DEPENDABLE AND HONEST
AND EASY TO MANIPULATE!

PECKHAM BOROUGH COUNCIL
HOUSING DEPARTMENT
TOWN HALL. PECKHAM.
LONDON SE15

17 August 1960

Mr and Mrs Clarence Tulser
Seaview Guest House
Sydenham Road
Peckham
London SE15

DENZIL WAS A GOOD-LOOKING LAD WHEN HE ARRIVED FROM LIVERPOOL

Dear Mr and Mrs Tulser

Following your visit to our office earlier today, I can confirm that you are now on the emergency housing list and that we will find a council house large enough for yourselves and your six sons as a matter of urgency.

In the meantime, the council will fund your B & B accommodation at the Seaview Guest House.

We understand from Liverpool City Council and Merseyside Police that the circumstances surrounding your departure from Liverpool and the criminal elements who believe that one or more of your sons may have been involved with one of more of their daughters, their daughters' mothers and possibly their daughters' aunts, make it impossible for you to return there.

We will keep you informed about when a suitable council house can be made available.

Yours sincerely

Henry Johnson

Henry Johnson
Housing Department

TRIGGER, ALBIE LITTLEWOOD AND DENZIL IN 1961

SOUTH LONDON HGV CENTRE
Queensmere Road, Peckham, London SE15

Denzil Tulser
11 Roseberry Hill
Peckham
London SE15

20 September 1968

Dear Denzil

I am pleased to enclose your certificate for passing our HGV driver's course. As the chief instructor on the course, I was most impressed with your handling of the various vehicles we used during your tuition, your roadcraft and your willingness to learn. You were an excellent pupil.

Please do drop in to see us from time to time to let us know how you are getting on. And if you see your friend any time soon - the one who was so keen to find out when you would be 'legit on the road' and to know 'how much gear' you could get in the back of the lorry - please tell him that the 'Genuine Rolex Lobster Perpetual' watch that he sold me has stopped.

Yours sincerely

Harry Bishop

Harry Bishop
Chief Examiner

SOUTH LONDON HGV CENTRE

The Driver Certificate of Professional Competence (Driver CPC) is a qualification for professional bus, coach and lorry drivers.

DENZIL'S WHEELS OVER THE YEARS
★ ★ ★ ★ ★ ★ ★ ★ ★ ★ ★ ★ ★ ★ ★ ★ ★ ★ ★

1985

1989

1992

2002

2005

Wedding Menu

Corinne and Denzil Tulser

Please make your selection from the buffet table

Lobster vol au vents

~~Game pie~~

Kidneys with saffron rice

Beef and anchovy savouries

Philadelphia truffles

Pie and chips all round!

followed by

~~Coffee or tea and a slice of the traditional three-tier wedding cake carved by the bride and groom~~

Jam Sponge

DENZIL'S TROUBLE AND STRIFE!

Denzil and his piles!

OUTPATIENTS DEPARTMENT

Peckham General Hospital
Denmark Hill
Peckham
London SE15

Mr Denzil Tulser
Flat 14
34 Peckham Road
Peckham
London SE15

Dear Mr Tulser

In your rush to leave the hospital this evening and get to the pharmacy, you left behind your repeat prescription form, which I have enclosed.

It is important that your continue to use the cream for the full period of two weeks. This will help to ease the stinging pain and also help to prevent any infection setting in.

It would also make sense for you to talk to your GP in order to be signed off work for at least a week. As a lorry driver, I imagine that you will have to spend long periods sitting down, and this may well tend to exacerbate your condition.

In future, we recommend that you take proper medical advice from a qualified physician before trying any kind of home remedy. As you now know, and despite any advice your friend Del may have given you, swollen and painful haemorrhoids do not respond well to being smeared with toothpaste.

Yours sincerely

Dr C Hutton

Dr C Hutton
Peckham General

Kingston upon Hull NHS
Psychiatric Evaluation Unit

PATIENT EVALUATION INTERVIEW

Subject: Denzil Tulser
Date of Birth: 08/08/1948
Place of Birth: Liverpool
Address: Flat 14, 34 Peckham Road, Peckham, London SE15

*Transcript of an interview conducted in December 1985
by Clinical Psychologist Dr Eileen Ruckwarts.*

Interviewer: How are you feeling today, Mr Tulser?

Subject: Fine, just a bit tired, you know. It ain't the same when you're not kipping in your own bed.

Interviewer: I am sure that we will be able to send you home soon, Mr Tulser. Can you tell me a little more about the voices you have been hearing? When do you hear them most?

Subject: I last heard them when I was driving my truck up here.

Interviewer: And what did they say?

Subject: Mainly, 'Stop the truck! Stop the truck! Pull over, you dipstick!' and some other stuff that I'd rather not repeat in front of a lady.

Interviewer: Would you say that this was an angry voice?

Subject: He was furious.

Seeing things in the mirror!

Hearing voices...

Seeing a Trotter at sea!

Interviewer: So it is a male voice?

Subject: Of course he's got a male voice.

Interviewer: And he tells you to do things?

Subject: It's more like he issues orders or commandments.

Interviewer: Would you ever consider not doing something he wanted you to do?

Subject: That's not possible. He makes you do stuff. You can't duck out of it.
                 He knows everything that goes on. He sees everything.

Interviewer: Would you say he was everywhere - omnipresent?

Subject: Too right I would. Everywhere, he is. Definitely omni-whatsit.

Interviewer: How do you know that he is everywhere?

Subject: Because I seen him, of course.

Interviewer: Where have you seen him?

Subject: Well, everywhere I go, really. At home in my flat, in the market,
                 in the Nag's Head, in the window of the cafe I stopped at up here.
                 When I was up on the cliffs I even saw him out at sea in a bright light.

Interviewer: Does he usually appear in bright silver or gold?

Subject: No. He usually appears in a canary yellow
                 three-wheeled van - a Reliant Regal.

Interviewer: God appears to you in a yellow Reliant Regal?

Subject: Not God, you divvy - Del!

Interviewer: Del? The Devil?

Subject: I wouldn't call him that, he's one of me best mates.

INTERVIEW TERMINATED.

Recommendation: *Further evaluation is essential to
establish the extent of the patient's delusions and
to find the underlying cause of his hallucinations.*

DENZIL FOUND OUT EVENTUALLY
HE WASNT REALLY SEEING THINGS!

DENZIL   197

THE DIARY OF JOAN TROTTER (PART 2)
★ ★

12 July 1961

My Freddie is a right laugh. He is very gentle, and tender and caring — not like any other man that I've ever met. When I go round his flat we always have a giggle. I once told him that, even though I had been working as his cleaning lady for months, I still had no idea how to switch his Hoover on. He said not to worry — there was one thing in the flat I always managed to turn on! I love him to bits, but it's awkward when he gives me money. Makes me feel like some kind of a call girl. But, as Freddie says, if I didn't take home me wages, Reg would get suspicious.

PASSIONATE TIMES WITH THE FROG

FREDDIE BROUGHT SO MUCH JOY TO MUM

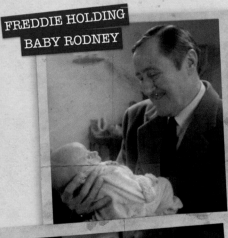

FREDDIE HOLDING BABY RODNEY

RODNEY COMING UP TO HIS FIRST BIRTHDAY

15 October 1962

Rodney is getting ever so big. No one in our family has ever been really tall but my boy is going to be a strapping six footer, just like his dad. Not Reg. Reg couldn't give a monkey's about him. Freddie cares, though. He tries to see Rodney every chance he gets. He says things like, "He's got my eyes, hasn't he? He's got my nose." And he does. Nobody else has noticed, but why should they? Nobody else except Renee knows about me and Freddie and, apart from me, the only one who pays any real attention to little Rodney is his brother, Del. Lovely Del. He dotes on his baby brother. What a sweetie!

24 October 1963

Freddie's dead! He's dead! Blown sky high robbing a post office in Plumstead! I can't believe it - I'm never going to see his lovely face again! I don't know if I can bear it. Apart from Rodney and Del, he was the only really good thing in my life. I've been in a right old state all day since I heard, but I've got to pull myself together. Del and Rodney still need me and I can't let them down. Freddie wouldn't want that and I know that he'll be up there looking down on me. From Heaven, that is, not from where he landed on the roof of the Bradford and Bingley. One day, Freddie, we will be in each other's arms again.

EMOTIONAL HUGS
WITH THE WONDER BABY

THE BEAUTIFUL
JOAN TROTTER
FELL ASLEEP
MARCH 12 1964

10 March 1964

Things have been getting a bit much for me lately. I don't seem to have the energy to keep my chin up no more. Truth be told, I'm not sure how much time I've got left. I might be seeing Freddie again sooner than I thought.

Del, I know that you will find all my scribblings and if you read this then I want you to know two things. The first is that you and Rodney always meant the world to me. I loved both my beautiful boys. The second - and I think that you've always known this - is that Rodney is your brother, but he's not Reg's son. You're a clever one, all right. Nobody can pull the wool over my Del's eyes, not even his own mum, so I know that you knew about Rodney and about me and Freddie. You've always cared for Rodney and you must always look after him. Share your dreams with him Del, and remember the wise words: 'You've got to have a dream - if you don't have a dream, how you gonna make a dream come true?'

Follow your dreams, Del, and this time next year, you'll be a millionaire.

CORNISH COURIER

Monday 15 October 1973

MAD AXEMAN MURDERS TOURISTS

A group of tourists has been murdered in their holiday cottage by an axe wielding maniac.

by Crime Reporter Robert Tregowan

The incident happened yesterday evening and local police were quickly on the scene following a 999 call from a woman in a neighbouring cottage who heard terrible screams coming from next door.

"It was awful," said Mrs Berlewen Tregowan. "It was early in the morning and I heard cursing and swearing like I haven't heard since my mother was alive. Then there was this awful screaming and somebody yelling, 'I love fish! I love fish!' That was when I phoned the police."

Local police responded immediately with Sergeant Iwan Tregowan racing to the incident in his new Triumph Dolomite patrol car. "When I arrived the suspect was outside the building wearing nothing but a brand new top hat and a pair of baggy Y-fronts. He was on the front lawn dancing round and round in little circles singing, 'I saved the little fishies' and waving an axe in the air. I circled round him and entered the building to check on the tourists but there was nothing I could do for them. I called for back-up and it took six of us to get him into a van."

By this time the local newsagent, Michael Tregowan, had arrived to deliver the latest *Cornish Courier*.

"It was awful," said Mr Tregowan,

Chief Inspector John Tregowan

"and a complete mystery really. I mean, where do you get a brand new top hat from around these parts?"

Cornish Police spokesman, Chief Inspector John Tregowan, said, "I can confirm that three tourists who had come to the area on a fishing trip were murdered last night. A man aged in his mid-thirties was taken into custody and is being held pending a psychiatric assessment."

Boycie's weekend cottage was in deepest Cornwall

HE'S A PSYCHO!

Rodders - you sure that wasn't a reflection!

Nothing like a trip to the outside loo in the rain!

TIME FOR SOME INVISIBLE SNOOKER!

CORNISH COURIER   Monday, 17 October 1983

ESCAPED AXE MURDERER CAPTURED

The notorious Cornish Axe Murderer escaped from Bodmin Moor High Security Prison on Friday but was recaptured with the help of a group of tourists.

BY CRIME REPORTER Nancy Tregowan

Charles "Chopper" Winters broke out of the prison when the security alarms were disabled during the storm that hit the area. During a temporary power cut he managed to overpower his guards in the darkness before the emergency generators had kicked in. Winters was then able to use their keys to release himself and scaled an outside wall topped with barbed wire to make his escape.

Winters then made his way across the moor to a cottage, often let to tourists, that was the scene of his brutal murder of three fishermen ten years ago.

By a strange quirk of fate, the cottage was occupied by three tourists who, just like those ten years ago, were on a weekend fishing trip.

"Well, I wouldn't exactly say we was doing any fishing," said Mr Derek Trotter, one of the tourists. "We was more thinking about a few river walks, and, if we could purchase the correct and pukka permits so as it was all kosher and above board, then we might have done a spot of angling. Maybe just a few salmons or trouts, perhaps a cod or haddock or two."

Mr Trotter was with his brother and Grandfather when Winters arrived at the cottage. Winters was dressed in the uniform of Chief Robson, head of security at the hospital. Winters hit him on the head and stole his uniform and identity papers.

"My brother let this geezer in," said Mr Trotter, "but straight away I could tell he weren't the full shilling. In my game, as an international entrepreneur, you have to be able to judge a character in an instant. It takes a certain 'Je nay say quack.' You either got it or you ain't. Well there was something iffy about this prison officer. He was definitely one lag short of a full wing."

Mr Trotter says that he helped his young brother and aged uncle to escape while he kept Winters occupied.

"He wanted to know if I liked fish and I said I loved them with a few chips and a bit of salt and vinegar and a glob of ta-ta. He weren't none too happy about that because he only liked fish that was alive and free to swim in the sea." explained Mr Trotter. "Well, I talked me way out of that one but next thing I knew, he wanted to play a game of snooker. Snooker, I ask you! You couldn't get a picnic table in that room, let alone a snooker table - but he said there was one right there in front of us. An invisible snooker table with invisible balls, all set up right there in the cottage.

"So he offered me a cue and we set to it. Seemed like a good way to kill time until the police arrived - and I would rather he was killing time than killing yours truly... Anyway, I'm no slouch on the old green beige. They used to call me the Steve Davison of Peckham. I played in an amateur tournament once against the Scotch champion, Hurricane Haggis.

"To make it all a bit more interesting, I offered him a tenner a frame. He seemed happy with that but he weren't that bothered about winning. He went in off the black twice. By the time the Old Bill got there we'd played three frames and I was thirty quid to the good - lovely jubbly!"

Mr Derek Trotter   Charles "Chopper" Winters

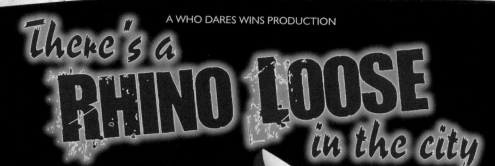

A WHO DARES WINS PRODUCTION

There's a RHINO LOOSE in the city

We should have another
go at this, Rodders.
I think I can still
get hold of a rhino.

SMASHING!!!
★★★★★
PECKHAM ECHO

WILD!!!
★★★★★
HOOKIE STREET MAGAZINE

A BLOCK BUSTER HORROR FEATURING A KILLER RHINO
ON A DEADLY RAMPAGE IN THE VERY HEART OF LONDON,
NO ONE IS SAFE!

BASED ON AN ORIGINAL IDEA BY JOHN SULLIVAN

WRITTEN BY
RODNEY TROTTER

STARRING
CHARLTON HESTON

DIRECTED BY
MICKEY PEARCE

SUPPORTING ARTISTS SUPPLIED BY THE TROTTER STAR AGENCY

THE ISLAND OF DEATH
Picture proposal by Derek E Trotter

The Island of Death is a pukka thriller starring Mel Gibson or, if we can't get him, possibly Harbinson Ford. I would play the lead role myself, but they will likely pull in more punters as they've done a few flicks already. Bums on seats is what it's all about, innit?

So the story starts on a tropical island what is supposed to be deserted and this bunch of boffins arrive on a boat to have a shuftie since there is strange volcanic stuff going on and they need to find out what's what.

Then some of the scientists' gofers start disappearing. These have got to be less important characters, expandable, like the geezers in the red shirts on Star Trek. The scientists, led by Mel Gibson and possibly me – I could make a brief appearance in a cameo role like that director bloke Albert Hitchcock always used to do – track the disappearances down to a series of caves, where they discover The Killer Cave Men.

Rodders was poncing about on Cassandra's lap top...

The Killer Cave Men, dressed in nothing but baggy Speedos and using spears and hatchets, attack the scientists and Mel Gibson is captured. He discovers that prisoners are being sacrificed to the god of the mountain by being lowered into a river of red-hot molten larva. He also discovers that there are Cave Women and has a fling with a good-looking sort that is sent to look after him. We should get that Myrtle Streep to play her. The cave women, of course, have a bit of covering up top, but not too much. We don't want a XXX certificate, but we want to see enough to keep it interesting.

Anyway, Mel Gibson and his tart are being lowered towards the larva on chains and he dips his chain into the larva and melts it so he can free himself and his cave woman. They are being chased when I appear and hold off the Killer Cave Men long enough for them to escape by blowing up the tunnel. This buries the cave men and me, so I die wiping out the cave men and plugging the larva that was causing all the volcanic ruptures.

.... I chipped in with some blinding creative plot ideas!

It's a winner – all you have to do is fill in a few gaps and write out all the speaking bits.

MIKE
★ ★ ★ ★ ★ ★

PROVIDER OF MANY A FINE BEVERAGE
THE EVER-DEPENDABLE MIKE!

PULLING PINTS IN PECKHAM

East End landlord Mike Fisher has just become the new landlord of The Nag's Head in Peckham and is over the moon to be involved with such a long-established business.

So what tempted Mike to head south of the river to Peckham.

"I had a great time in my previous pub," said Mike, "but working your way up from barman to publican takes a lot of hours. My missus at the time chucked me out. Said that if I liked spending more time at the pub than I did with her, then I could go and live there. So I did, and I've never looked back."

Mike is settling in to the Nag's Head, finding ways to put his own stamp on the premises without alienating the pub's regulars.

"It's great that the locals regard The Nag's Head as 'their' boozer, not mine," said Mike, "but I have managed to make a few small changes without upsetting anyone. The brewery paid for the bar to be redecorated and I had a local contractor come in to do that for me at a very reasonable rate."

The Nag's Head locals can be quite colourful characters, as Mike has discovered.

"We've got on old boy who comes in, has a couple of half pints and a shot of navy rum, then insists on playing the piano," said Mike. "He can bash out a tune alright, but not everyone wants to hear it. Then he starts singing songs from the war and some people get a bit shirty with him - especially when he sings What Shall We Do With The Drunken Sailor for the seventh or eighth time. I've tried threatening to ban him and all sorts, but he just laughs and sits there in his duffel coat, supping his half pint with crisps in his beard. I can't be too hard on him, really, and his nephew is a good mate who's always out to do me a favour or two . . . at a price."

Does that mean that Mike sees himself staying in Peckham?

"Without a doubt. Nothing could persuade me to leave here now that I've settled in. Peckham is the crème de la menthe, as one of my

3

Mike and Eddie Chambers, an old Eastend Pub rival.

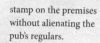

MEETING MIKE FOR THE VERY FIRST TIME

Peckham General Hospital
Muamar Gaddafi Road • Peckham • London SE15
Accident and Emergency Department Incident Report

Name: Michael Fisher

Address: Nag's Head, Peckham High Street, Peckham

Type of injury: Painful

Cause of injury: My own stupidity

Describe how the injury was sustained:

I had just had my breakfast and I was drying my hair. I ain't got a lot of hair, but I like to try to look my best when I'm serving behind the bar. Well, you've got to make an effort, ain't you?

Then I caught a sniff of what smelled like bacon cooking. Course, I thought "You must have left some bacon in the pan, you pillock." Then I remembered that I'd had scrambled eggs that morning not bacon. Then I felt the heat and I realised that it wasn't bacon that was cooking, it was my own head!

It turned out that the hair dryer I had bought off a mate was not a hair dryer at all. It was a hot air gun for stripping paint. Well, there was no paint to deal with but it made short work of stripping a layer of skin off my head.

At first, I thought "That's the last time I buy anything off that Del Trotter" but actually, it will come in handy when I'm doing up my bathroom and it were a really good price. So, the hairdryer ain't a problem, but my head is.

How did you get to the hospital?:
I legged it here balancing a bag of ice on my bonce.

Do you have a friend or relative who can take you home after treatment?:
No, but if I'm not back behind the bar at lunchtime, they'll be in there helping themselves.

Do you have any allergies or other complaints that could effect your treatment?:
No, but I don't just want a little bandage. I want a bloody great big one wrapped right round my head.

Mike bit my hand off for a new hair dryer!

Sadly the wally took it too far - and burnt his head!

MIKE PUT ON A GREAT SPREAD FOR UNCLE ALBERT'S BIRTHDAY PARTY IN 1988

MIKE WAS ALWAYS UP FOR BUYING A NEW GIZMO!

Mike faxed us about a mystery reunion...

...and he was none the wiser as to who organised it!

FAX MESS§§MASSAGE§§§MESSAG§§§§§

FROM: Mike
Fischerrrrrrrrrrrrrrrrrrrrrrrrrrrrrrrrrr

AT: Nog's Heed Pubic Mouse

TO: Del Trottttttttttttttttttttttttt^%
AT: TIT-TIT-TIT-TITcorrrrrrrrrrrrrrrS!!!§

Machine not wor3333 PROP@@d@@erluuu.
BugG33!!!!!!!

Bloke wants you to ‡‡‡‡ll‡‡‡l‡+‡‡‡
school4444444444 reunion for <<< Martin
Luther King Commmmmmmmmmmprohesive
Class of 199999999999999999999962.

It's tonight her at the Noooogs Had.

And can we toooooooooolk about this
bloooooooooô22œy machiiiiiiine?

                    Milke

WHEN WE BECAME MILLIONAIRES, MIKE GOT A ROUND OF CHAMPAS ON THE HOUSE!

THE HOTEL CASTANETS

Alicante, Spain

Dear Mike

Buenos Dias from sunny Spain. Only here for one night before I move on but thought it would be a good idea to drop you a line.

Fine times we had in Peckham, eh? I'll never forget those overnight trips to sign off your accounts. Wine and ale and whisky and champagne. Well, if you're in the trade you have to sample the goods to know what your talking about, eh? Speaking of sampling the goods, that Foxy Thigh-High was something special. Pity I won't be around to see any more of her - although I think we saw pretty much all there was to see of her and her friend Melons Merryjingle. What a Christmas Eve that was.

Reason that I won't be seeing them, or you, again is that I've had to make myself scarce. I suggest you think about doing the same thing, mate. The auditors have started trawling through those dodgy accounts of ours and they will eventually find all that dosh we salted away. Best get your mitts on the cash from wherever you stashed it and go to ground, eh?

I guess we won't be seeing each other again, so goodbye Mike. It was a blast.

Johnno

Mike ran a 'guess the baby Trotter' name competition.

MIKE WITH TRIG AT THE 1989 JOLLY BOYS' OUTING

LAST BELL FOR PECKHAM LANDLORD

Popular publican Mike Fisher is now doing time instead of calling time after he was caught by Home Counties Brewers and Distillers doing a little distilling of his own - siphoning cash from the company's accounts.

LANDLORD OF THE NAG'S HEAD IN PECKHAM, Fisher has been handed a prison sentence after he and a former HCBD employee fiddled returns, receipts and VAT figures to cream off thousands from the company. The exact figure has yet to be determined but a source at HCBD said, "We are uncovering more irregularities all the time but the figure is in the tens of thousands at least."

Acting with his accomplice, believed to be former HCBD accountant Jonathan "Johnno" Johnson, the money was embezzled over a protracted period. Johnson's whereabouts are currently unknown.

Fisher is thought to have invested the embezzled cash in the Central American Stock Market on the advice of friends. When the market crashed, he lost everything and defrauded the brewery of even more money to try to recoup his losses.

'I thought this would be a way to finally get myself a little nesteg for the future," Fisher said in his defence. "I know it was wrong and I shouldn't have listened to the plonkers who told me to put all the money in that Central American scheme. I'm sorry for all the trouble I've caused."

The Nag's Head was closed for just one day before HCBD were able to appoint a new publican to take over the business. Local cafe owner

Sid Robertson is now the pub's new landlord, but putting Robertson in charge was not a popular decision with all of the locals

"How can they put a pillock like that in charge of The Nag's Head?" said regular Albert Trotter. "They serve food in that pub and he's been done over and over again for serving dodgy food. He's called the Peckham Poisoner. He's put more people in hospital than the Krays!"

In response to this criticism, Mr Robertson said: "He's barred."

Sadly, Mr Trotter, a colourful local character, died just a few days ago, although his passing is not thought to have anything to do with the food served in The Nag's Head.

Above: *Seeing the funny side – Locals with new Landlord Sid Robertson (Far Left)*

ON THE SLATE

THE NAG'S HEAD

High Street, Peckham, London SE15

INVOICE

<u>Funeral of Edward Trotter</u>

Hire of glasses etc...	free of charge
Sherry, wine, spirits and other drinks etc...	£86
Sandwiches and sausage rolls	£30

Total: £116

*Potpourri, Mike, potpourri.
You really know how to kick a man when he's
down. You must leave us all to grieve and seek
closure before we can deal with this... You'll be
offering a discount for cash next – won't ya?*

*Elsie Partridge created
quite an atmosphere!*

*Mike did Rodders and Cass
proud on their big day.*

THE NAG'S HEAD

High Street, Peckham, London SE15

INVOICE

<u>Hosting the wedding of Rodney Trotter and Cassandra Parry</u>

Hire of premises	free of charge

And even that's too bloody expensive!

120 pints of lager	£129.60
97 pints of bitter	£95.06

Beer was watered down by at least 20%, so we'll call that £175

20 bottles of Champagne	£400

*Leave it out, Mike! We know you was topping up with Asti
Spumucho, so you can have 200 quid for that*

10 bottles of whisky	£100
10 bottles of gin	£70

*And you can cut your mark-up off these,
cos I flogged em to you! Make it £95*

Variety of soft drinks and mixers	£40

£25 – mate's rates!

50 bowls of jellied eels	£50
Finger buffet	£120

*A fair price for the jellied eels and they was excellent, but
everything else on the buffet also tasted of jellied eels on
account of it all being kept in the same fridge for too long,
so we'd best knock a score off that – call it £150.*

Hire of disco	£100

DJ did not have 'Old Shep' so I am deducting a tenner – £90.

Total: £1,104.66

*With my slight adjustments that is actually a far more
reasonable £735. I would settle up but it is the privilege of the
father of the bride to pay for this, so stick it on a tab for Alan
Parry and he'll see you right next time he's in.*

THE NAG'S HEAD
High Street, Peckham, London SE15
INVOICE
Birthday Party for Albert Trotter

Drinks at bar   £235
Sandwiches etc...   £125

Total: £360

I don't see why I should stump up for this lot. I never even got near a sandwich because the Old Bill dragged me off down the nick! I'll have a whip round them what scoffed it all and run up the bar bill and we can sort this next week!

THE NAG'S HEAD
High Street, Peckham, London SE15
INVOICE
Séance with Elsie Partridge

Hire of function room   £30
Brandy consumed following séance   £45
1 x porkpie   50p

Total: £75.50

Del's comment: Be fair, Mike. We all needed something to calm our nerves after that performance. I hardly touched a drop due to me dicky tummy. It was Boycie that was knocking it back. You should stick this one on his tab. Anyway, how can you have a seance if there's no spirits involved? Ha-ha!

THE NAG'S HEAD
High Street, Peckham, London SE15
INVOICE
For hosting Dockside Secondary Modern Class of '62 Reunion.

Hire of function room   £30
Beer, wines and spirits   £70
Sandwiches and cup cakes   £25

Total: £125

Be serious, Mike! You can't expect me to cop for this one - Roy Slater was the one who organised it all. You'll have to track him down if you want this paying. Try turning over a few rocks, he might come crawling out.

Del, this is everything you've had me chalk up on the slate for you since the start of last month. I really need you to settle this urgently. I was going to put prices on here and add it up but the calculator you gave me made a 'pop' sound and now it has smoke coming out of it.

Can we talk about this and work out how much you owe, please?

Mike

6 x banana daiquiris
10 x Singapore slings
2 x Caribbean stallions
10 x non-alcoholic lager-tops
8 x navy rums
2 x Campari and cherryades
12 x packs ready salted peanuts
4 x bacon sandwich
(with red and brown sauce)

Happy to enter into negotiations on this Mike. I should say that the Caribbean stallions had so little actual alcohol in them that they were more like geldings than stallions. And you have to stop letting Albert stick his drinks on my tab! As regards the calculator, that was on approval, sale or return. If you've toasted it, you can't return it, can you? So we'll start by knocking the cost of that off the tab. I should be in tomorrow night when we can work our way through this ... and then start with a clean slate!)

WAR DEPARTMENT

ARMY FORM No 1579

POW REPATRIATION REPORT

FULL NAME AND SERVICE NUMBER:
PRIVATE SIDNEY R BERTS   N 8410932

REGIMENT:
MIDDLESEX REGIMENT

SID PICTURED
AT THE 1960
JOLLY BOYS'
OUTING!

PART ONE - DESCRIBE HOW YOU ESCAPED FROM ENEMY CUSTODY:

We was being held on a Greek island called Siros. the Germans marched us from the docks to the camp where we was allocated tents.
After a few days we was set to work, some of us unloading boats at the quayside. That made it easy for us to trade stuff like army belts and boots for bottles of the local plonk called Rotsina. It was dreadful muck but it packed a punch and we traded that with the German guards at the camp for more food.

Then, when the guards had all had a skinful of the Rotsina one afternoon, we just walked out of the camp. We posed as a working party at the docks and had halfinched a torpedo boat before anyone knew what was happening. We had one bloke knew how to start it up and steer it and we was off. They can't half shift, those torpedo boats. We was miles out at sea before any of the Krauts cottoned on.

Then we came across this Greek fishing boat, but when we got close, it turned towards us and rammed us. Well, our boat went down quicker than a two bob tart.

Funny thing is, when they steamed past all of us splashing about in the water, it sounded like they was shouting at us in English. A bit cockney even. The pillock steering the Greek boat yelled at me, "Tell Aydolf that he's funnier than Charlie Chaplin" and then he called me a 'puddenfaced sausage muncher." They thought we was German. We was screaming at them in English but they couldn't hear us. Most of them was too busy singing a song about how Hitler is one nut short of a full sack.

So we was left clinging to the wreckage for a few hours until a Royal Navy destroyer came by and picked us all up.

UNCLE ALBERT AND SID OFTEN
REMINISCED ABOUT THE WAR...

SID NEARLY ALWAYS HAS
A FAG IN HIS MOUTH

SID   213

PECKHAM COUNCIL ENVIRONMENTAL HEALTH DEPARTMENT

Food Hygiene (Commercial Premises) Division
Town Hall, Peckham, London SE15

ENFORCEMENT NOTICE - CLOSURE OF PREMISES

Mr Sidney Robertson
Old Oak Cafe
High Street
Peckham
London SE15

12 March 1981

Dear Mr Robertson

This letter is your formal notice that, following a recent inspection of your premises by an accredited Peckham Council Food Hygiene Officer, the Old Oak Cafe has failed to meet minimum hygiene standards on every possible count.

There were many contraventions of regulations regarding the storage, cooking and serving of food to the public (all such contraventions listed on a Addendum A attached) but whilst on your premises the inspector was alarmed to see:

1. Cigarette ash on buttered toast being served to a customer

2. A large green slug that had fallen into a pot of beans and was cooking on the surface

3. Food stored in the kitchen area that was up to four years beyond its 'use by' date

4. Droppings from rats and mice in the vicinity of stored food

5. Evidence of rats and mice having gnawed their way into stored food packaging

6. Actual rats and mice eating stored food

The inspector has since been off work recovering after hospital treatment for the rodent bites sustained during his inspection of your premises.

YOU ARE INSTRUCTED TO CLOSE THE ROYAL
OAK CAFE WITH IMMEDIATE EFFECT

The premises must remain closed to the public until you have taken steps to remedy all of the contraventions of regulations listed on Addendum A and the premises have been re-inspected to ensure that all necessary remedial action has been taken.

Your sincerely

C Grimsdale

Mr C Grimsdale

SLATER - THE HATED COPPER USED SID'S CAFE TO TRY AND RECURIT INFORMANTS

Sid once accused me of nicking cutlery!

Metro Cafe
(formerly the Royal Oak)
High Street
Peckham
London SE15

19 March 1981

Mr C Grimsdale
Chief Environmental Health Officer
Peckham Council
Town Hall
Peckham
London SE15

Dear Mr Grimsdale

I have given the old cafe the once over and it is now ready for one of your inspectors again. It's had a bit of clean up, a lick of paint and I've given it a new name. Got rid of the rodents in the kitchen, too.

I should point out a few things about your inspector's last visit, though

1. That might not have been fag ash, it could have been pepper as I have a couple of regulars like their butter a bit peppery to take the sour taste away.

2. That was not a green slug in the bowls, it was a gherkin.

3. The out of date food is gone, although there was nothing wrong with it. It has been much more than four years since that whole listeria fiasco.

4. I have many talents, but training rats and mice to use the toilet facilities ain't one of them.

5. The rats and mice only gnawed their way in on account of the fact that their little hands ain't strong enough to tear the tops off the cardboard boxes.

6. The rats and mice was only eating my grub because they had fled from the Chinese restaurant two doors down where even the rodents won't eat the muck they serve.

Don't send that inspector what got bitten. It took me hours to clean the blood off the sausages. He's barred. Send someone else quick as you like so I can open up and get all my regular punters back in again.

Yours sincerely

Sidney Robertson

QUICK CROSSWORD

Clues

Across

1. A word teamed with back
3. Transport
7. She's got Bette Davis …
8. Flames can do this
9. Prisoners dream of this

Down

2. Goes with 1 across
4. A dangerous job
5. It's a diamond
6. There's nothing like it

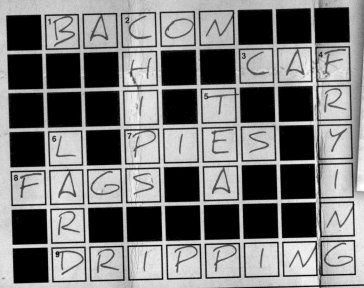

ME AND DENZIL
PICK SID'S BRAIN

SID OFF-DUTY ON THE 1989
JOLLY BOYS' OUTING

QUICK CROSSWORD ANSWERS

Old Oak Cafe
under new management as

It's still Sid – he's just gone and got a new pot washer

METRO
SID'S CAFÉ

Return of The Fatty Thumb

Sid has been feeding the Trotter's for decades!

Breakfast - Served All Day

You'll likely see it again by lunchtime anyway!

Full English: £2.99
Sausage, bacon, beans, bubble and squeak, black pudding, mushrooms, fried egg, fried bread, fried tomato, tea, toast.

And you will!

Half English: £1.99 — *Half Alien*
Sausage, bacon, fried egg, beans, tea, toast.

Quarter English: £1.50
Sausage, bacon, beans, tea

Lunch - Served All Afternoon

Pie, chips, beans, bread and butter, tea - £2.99

Pie, chips, beans, tea - £2.50

Brewed with fag ends and strained through seldom laundered Y-fronts

Pie, chips, tea - £2.00

But only if the pie man's been

Pie, tea - £1.50

Pie - £1.00

Never seen any service around here!

SERVICE NOT INCLUDED

ANOTHER BUSY MORNING AT SID'S CAFE!

Ridgemere Hall

I remember this gaff. I sold em a musical cat but they never coughed up the readies. Said they never carried cash.

Nestling in the Kent countryside, deep in the heart of the 'Garden of England' is one of the finest grand houses in the South East – Ridgemere Hall.

The Trotter family arrive!

The majority of the house dates back to 1642, although the house was gradually expanded throughout the 17th and 18th centuries. The extensive grounds and gardens have recently been restored to the way they would have looked when they were originally laid out by Capability Brown, but it is the house itself that is the jewel in the estate's crown.

Ridgemere Hall has been in the possession of the Ridgemere family since it was built – one of the few homes of substance in England from this period that is still owned and occupied by the family that first built it.

"I have never lived anywhere else and could never contemplate leaving Ridgemere," said the present occupant, Lord Horatio Ridgemere, who shares the family pile with his wife, Lady Elizabeth. "It has been my family's home for almost 400 years and there is

Above: The 17th century chandelier.

18

nowhere in the world I would rather be. I just wish that more people could share this magnificent and important part of our country's history."

And now, of course, we all can, as the house and grounds have recently been opened to the public.

Ridgemere Hall emerges through the trees as you approach on the long driveway up to the house. Parking is easy in the newly-constructed car park just a short stroll from the massive oak front door.

On entering the house, you walk into the fabulous main hall, where your eye is drawn to the beautiful plasterwork on the ceiling and a breathtaking 150-piece chandelier.

"The chandelier is very special," said Lord Ridgmere. "Priceless and beautiful. It is Louis 14th – hand cut 17th century crystal. We did have two, but one became a 150,000 piece chandelier when some numbskulls dropped it while it was being cleaned."

The incident is still painful for Lord Horatio to recall. "We were in the West Wing Drawing Room having tea when we heard the crash," he remembers. "By the time we rushed down to find out what had happened, the contractors had fled."

"The chandelier itself was irreplaceable," said Lord Horatio, "but the insurance settlement allowed us to finish restoring the house and gardens in order to make them available to the general public."

Not only are the house and gardens now open between April and October, but you can also enjoy a fine dining experience with Lord and Lady Ridgemere in the banqueting room of Ridgemere Hall, served by Lord Ridgemere's faithful butler, Wallace, who, Lord Horatio jokes, 'has been here since the house was built!' During the meal, Lord Horatio and Lady Elizabeth will chat with you about the history of the hall and some of their colourful ancestors. ●

Entrance to the house and gardens costs £25 per person.

Dinner at Ridgemere Hall (max 8 persons) cost £125 per head.

Numbskulls!! That's us he's talking about!

That crumbly old git of a butler told us they was on holiday! I smell a rat! They would have dodged payin up for that job!

Above: Loyal butler - Wallace

I knew it! They was totally skint! We'd never have got paid!

Grandad - Don't!

£125 for a bit of scoff! You could buy enough lobster vindaloo to feed the whole of Peckham for that price! What a bunch of rip-off artists. You just can't trust them Aristocats.

Above: Lord Horatio Ridgemere

Above: Lady Elizabeth

Right - time we scarper!

ROY SLATER

★ ★ ★ ★ ★ ★ ★ ★ ★ ★

POLICE CADET SLATER
IN DECEMBER 1960

SLATER AN UNWELCOME GUEST
IN THE TROTTER FLAT IN 1983

Dockside Secondary Modern School
Peckham, London, SE15

School Report *June 1961*

Name: *Roy Slater*

Form: *Class 11c*

Head Teacher's comments:

Roy is one of those boys - and there are precious few like him - who is never late for school and always arrives neatly turned out in more or less the correct school uniform unless he has been waylaid on his journey to school by some of his more obstreperous classmates. Sadly, when their horseplay becomes overly boisterous it tends to be Roy who ends up in a puddle or with his blazer on the roof of a bus heading for Acton. He can always be relied upon, however, to tell us exactly who the culprits were when this happens and indeed, when any other incidents arise during school time, whether he is involved or not

Subject Grades:
Subject	Grade
English	A
Arithmetic	A
Mathematics	B
Chemistry	B
Biology	B
Physics	C
Geography	B
History	A
Art	C
Woodwork & Metalwork	C

Head Teacher's Comments on Grades:

Roy's grades have improved this year, although some of his teachers seem reluctant to explain how he has achieved this. They deny outright that he has had any undue influence over their marking of his test papers but he seems a little smug and they do tend to shy away from him, as though he may know something about them that he shouldn't.

Summary:

Roy regards himself as a cut above the rest of his contemporaries - more astute, more intelligent, more trustworthy and more highly regarded by his teachers. He is wrong, of course, but it may take him years to realise that. The other boys tend to be utterly dishonest rogues and can be relied upon to behave as such at all times. Roy tends only to look after himself and seems to have a darker side. This will not hinder him from leaving school as one of our highest academic achievers, which will doubtless only serve to make him less popular than he is already.

PECKHAM'S YOUNGEST COP MAKES FIRST ARREST

He may still be wet behind the ears, but Peckham's youngest police officer has made his first arrest on his first day on the job.

POLICE CADET ROY SLATER was wandering through Peckham Market in an off-duty moment when he spotted bargain records on sale at prices that were too good to be true.

"In fact," said Cadet Slater, "they were clearly too good to be legal. No import duties or other taxes had been paid and the two villains who were selling the records were obviously not licensed market traders."

Cadet Slater moved in on the pair and took them into custody along with their illicit goods. He could not confirm what then happened to the crooks.

"I just handed them in," said Cadet Slater. "It's not up to me what happens next, but I would throw the book at them. I won't stand for that sort of thing on my patch!"

When asked if he would receive a commendation for his actions, a police spokesman said: "Oh, Slater will get what's coming to him all right."

SLATER'S MUM DESPISED ROY NEARLY AS MUCH AS HIS OLD MAN!

Roy, you little runt!

I can't believe the grief you've put me through. They kept me for hours down at that police station asking me all sorts of questions about things that have got bugger all to do with them.

This was all your fault. I mean, who goes about arresting people for having a dodgy rear light on their bike? It's the kind of thing you point out to someone to be helpful, not the sort of thing you nick them for! What makes it worse is that you lent me the bleedin' bike in the first place!

I will never speak to you again.

YOU'RE NO SON OF MINE.

Dad

PECKHAM POLICE
Suspect Observation and Surveillance Report

Surveillance Officer: PC Roy Slater
Suspect: Derek Edward Trotter
Location: 127 Sir Walter Raleigh House, New World Estate, Peckham, London SE15

7.30 am
Subject appeared outside the door to his flat and entered the lift. I followed him down via the stairs.

7.33 am
I arrived on the ground floor in time to see the subject re-enter the lift and head for the 12th floor. I followed via the stairs.

7.37 am
I arrived on the 12th floor in time to see the subject re-enter the lift and head for the ground floor. I followed via the stairs.

7.40 am
I arrived on the ground floor in time to see the subject re-enter the lift and head for the sixth floor. I followed via the stairs.

7.42 am
I arrived on the sixth floor in time to see the subject re-enter the lift and head for the ground floor. I followed via the stairs.

7.45 am
The subject finally left the building, heading for Peckham High Street on a bicycle. I followed on foot.

7.50 am
On reaching the High Street, I observed the subject heading down Dock Lane. I followed on foot.

7.55 am
From the end of Dock Lane, I observed the subject heading along Shore Street and turning up Canal Road back towards the High Street. I followed on foot.

8.00 am
The subject entered the Royal Oak Cafe and proceeded to the counter. I entered and sat by the door.

8.02 am
The subject walked towards me from the counter and put a cup of tea in front of me, saying, "You'll be needing this by now, Roy." He then went outside and swapped his bicycle for an accomplice's Lambretta before making off.

8.03 am
Surveillance terminated.

SLATER'S PATHETIC
SURVEILLANCE PHOTOS

PECKHAM POLICE
MEMO

Date: 25 March 1977

From: Chief Superintendent White

To: Detective Sergeant Slater

Subject: Your Recent Promotion Board

I have to tell you that you have been unsuccessful in your application for promotion to Inspector.

There were some irregularities concerning your Inspector's Exam. The official invigilator during the written exam recalled you as a slim blond-haired young man with a moustache. This gives grounds for suspicion that it may not actually have been you who sat the test.

Furthermore, reports have surfaced about the stolen police vehicle - an unmarked Ford Cortina - that you apparently 'recovered' in Dover. It was witnessed being driven in Calais, Lyon and St Tropez by a man fitting your description. The obvious conclusion is that the driver actually was you and I will be launching a full inquiry.

Allegations have also emerged about your relationships with local traders and shopkeepers. It has been said that you may have let it be known that you would 'turn a blind eye' to irregularities in return for cash and services. Again, an inquiry will determine whether you should face a disciplinary hearing.

M White.

Chief Superintendent White
Peckham Police Station

SUPERINTENDENT WHITE, SLATER'S FORMER BOSS

TRIG TRIES TO WARN RODDERS TO KEEP HIS TRAP SHUT!

Slater was hated by both old bill and us lot.

As bent a copper you'll ever find!

Dear Chalky

A bloke could get really offended when his boss writes him a memo like this. Quite frankly, I'm hurt that you could think such things about me. After all, we're not all perfect are we? Not even you. In fact, 'especially not you....

I think that you might want to go back to the promotion board and recommend that they reconsider my promotion. Otherwise, your wife might get to hear about that little flat you rent above the dry cleaner's in Lambeth. She'll wonder what that's all about, won't she?

And I don't think you really want to go launching an inquiry into that old Ford Cortina, do you? Otherwise, your wife might want to know why your own car is parked outside that dry cleaners in Lambeth every Tuesday and Thursday night when you're supposed to be working the late shift.

And my dealings with informants and the general public on my patch are of concern only to me - so there's no need for you to go poking your nose in there, either, is there? Otherwise, your wife might get to see a few snaps I have of you and your friend in Lambeth - Felicity, or Foxy Thigh-High as she is known in the trade.

I will be around later for a chat. If not with you, then with Mrs White. I'm sure she loves to hear stories about policemen. She is the Chief Constable's daughter, after all.

Your friend Roy

1977

PECKHAM POLICE
Suspect Observation and Surveillance Report

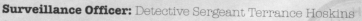

Surveillance Officer: Detective Sergeant Terrance Hoskins
Suspect: Chief Inspector Roy Slater
Location: Nag's Head public house, Peckham, London, SE15

12.15 pm
Arrived at the premises with the subject and DC Parker.

12.32 pm
The subject, still wearing a sombrero from an attempt to blend with homecoming tourists at the airport, burst into the back room of the premises. We had drawn a blank at the airport and it was to become evident that the diamonds had been smuggled in by sea. DC Parker and I covered the other exits.

12.33 pm
The subject addressed five men in the room where a quantity of cash was visible, ready to be traded for the diamonds. The men were Aubrey Boyce, a male known only as Abdul, Derek Trotter, Rodney Trotter and another male disguised as Captain Birdseye.

12.34 pm
The subject ordered DC Parker and I to withdraw and continued his conversation with the five men. From my vantage point in the hallway, I overheard the subject remonstrating with the five men and offering to make sure that no charges were brought against them in return for them giving him the diamonds. That's when I knew that we had him. The whole lot was on my hidden tape recorder.

12.38 pm
The subject was recorded boasting about how he and an accomplice in Amsterdam, a Mr Van Cleef, had duped several other victims into smuggling diamonds into the country for them, making a fortune while others took the risks. He then 'confiscated' the gems when they arrived in England. The tape machine then made a high pitched squeak like a hamster on helium and I knew I needed to insert a new tape. This is not easy when the machine is fastened to your inside thigh and I recommend that in future it be hidden somewhere else about the operator's person.

12.44 pm
The subject left the back room. He gave me a funny look when he caught me with my hands down by trousers, then ordered me to accompany him to his car. I was acting as his driver.

12.47 pm
The subject sat in the passenger seat and intimated that there were no diamonds recovered during the raid. Everything that he said was still being recorded via the tape machine's hidden microphone in my lapel.

12.50 pm
I drove the subject to a pre-arranged roadblock where he realised that he had, in fact, been the subject of a covert surveillance operation and was about to be arrested.

12.55 pm
The subject pleaded with me and offered substantial amounts of money to get him out of the situation. A certain odour led me to believe that he may have been suffering from his old stomach trouble again.

12.56 pm
Surveillance Terminated

Not a welcome surprise!

We all thought we woz done for!

At last Slater is about to get banged-up!

PECKHAM COP JAILED

A Peckham police officer once commended for making an arrest on his first day as a policeman, was jailed today for corruption and diamond smuggling.

Disgraced former Chief Inspector Roy Slater will be sentenced next week but is expected to spend the next five years behind bars. Slater was the subject of a police 'sting' operation but there was no shortage of witnesses willing to take the stand against him

One character witness surprised the court by describing him as: "A despicable, back-stabbing, heartless, disloyal, untrustworthy, dishonest, lying, cheating piece of shit." Harsh words indeed from Mrs Ruby Slater, the defendant's mother. "He drove my poor Harry to his grave," said Mrs Slater, referring to the defendant's father.

Suspicions about the way Slater conducted his investigations were aroused when he arrested a man who confessed to being a 'Peeping Tom' who liked to watch women through the windows

of their own homes. Once in court it transpired that the man was registered blind.

The surveillance operation that led to Slater's arrest uncovered his involvement in a diamond smuggling racket. When the trial reached the point where Slater's assistant, Detective Sergeant Hoskins, was giving evidence against his old boss, it seemed that proceedings might have to be halted as the drains below Peckham Crown Court appeared to be backed up.

A note was passed from DS Hoskins to the Judge who asked the accused, "Is it the old stomach complaint again, Mr Slater?" When the jury retired to consider their verdict, the foreman announced that they were refusing to return until someone opened a window.

On hearing the 'guilty' verdict, there was shouting, whistling and cheering from the public gallery, although Mrs Slater was eventually dragged out by security guards.

MARGATE MESSENGER

16P

TUESDAY 29 AUGUST 1989

COACH EXPLODES IN BALL OF FLAMES

A group of day-trippers were lucky to escape with their lives when their coach burst into flames on the Canterbury Road yesterday.

As the Fire Brigade fought to bring the blaze under control, traffic began to tail back in all directions, turning the usual Bank Holiday traffic chaos into complete gridlock. When they were eventually able to get inside the coach, Sub-Officer Sam Payne said the cause of the blaze was clear.

"The way that the fire spread and the seat of the blaze indicate that the fire started under the dashboard. A recently fitted radio cassette player appears to have overheated, eventually catching fire. Proximity to the fuel lines brought about a rapid expansion of the fire."

Flames were reported to be shooting up to 30 feet in the air and the fire left most of the coach party so shocked that they immediately hurried back inside the pub for a stiff drink.

"I never seen anything like it in all my years at the wheel," said coach driver Harry Styles. "I was feeling really groggy when we stopped at the pub on the way down here so that the lads could all have a drink. I think it must have been fumes from that radio before it finally went up."

Police were quickly on the scene, trying to divert the heavy traffic away from the area, but tailbacks still extended all the way to the sea front with side roads becoming blocked.

"Even once the Fire Brigade had the situation under control and the coach had been made safe it was difficult to get traffic moving again," admitted Inspector Kevin Ansett. "Traffic congestion made it difficult to bring in a recovery vehicle large enough to clear the wreckage. Many motorists suffered lengthy delays. My wife was late for bingo. She was livid."

MUSTA 20W
CAR RADIO CASSETTE PLAYER
IN-CAR AUDIO

Inspector Ansett warned that this may not be an isolated incident.

"There have been reports of these particular radio cassettes, the Musta F80 model manufactured in Albania **(Below)**, causing problems for motorists all over the south east of England," said Inspector Ansett. "We would warn drivers who have had these units fitted not to switch them on. If you have one in your car, disconnect it immediately and remove it from the vehicle.

"The toxic fumes emitted as these radio cassettes heat up can easily overpower a driver, causing drowsiness, a sensation similar to alcoholic intoxication and short-term memory loss. No one, for example, seems to be able to remember where they bought their Musta F80. You should certainly not drive your car with one of these things wired up."

Police are keen to talk to anyone who has suffered any after effects from the fitting of a Musta F80 in their vehicle, especially if they can shed any light on the source of these devices.

Denzil puckering up to Boycie!

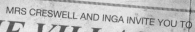

MRS CRESWELL AND INGA INVITE YOU TO

THE VILLA BELLA
GUEST HOUSE
12a, Granville Parade, Margate

ALL ROOMS £10 A NIGHT PER PERSON
(INCLUDES A TRADITIONAL ENGLISH BREAKFAST)

PLEASE NOTE:

DOORS LOCKED AT 11PM,

NOT OPENED AGAIN UNTIL 9AM

Belly-aching laughs
with all my mates

A WONDERFUL DAY IN MARGATE...

...COMPLETE WITH A LOBSTER VINDALOO AND 14 PINA COLADAS!

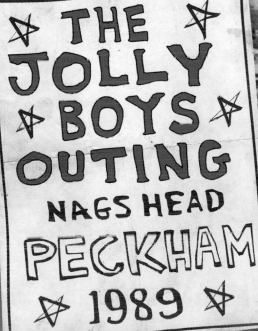

★ THE JOLLY BOYS OUTING NAGS HEAD PECKHAM 1989 ★

THE DRISCOLL BROTHERS

DANNY AND TONY DRISCOLL

DON'T EVER CALL THEM

LITTLE AND LARGE!

GANGSTERS OF LONDON

By Colin Wolf

Chapter 12

THE DRISCOLL BROTHERS

The Driscoll Brothers, Danny and Tony, were the sons of Bill Driscoll, a petty thief who once worked as a stable hand in a mansion owned by a very wealthy family. Following a fire at the house, Bill was accused of stealing jewellery and was arrested. His sons always maintained that their father was the victim of a grave injustice. "He was stitched up," Tony once said. "They had nothing on him – no evidence whatsoever. Apart from the fingerprints. And the eyewitnesses. And the jewels they found in his pocket. Apart from that they had nothing!" Bill Driscoll's time in custody ended in a police cell when he died in what the police described as 'a botched suicide attempt'. Given that he did die, however, it is hard to see how it could be described as 'botched'. Police claimed that he tried to hang himself with his braces and fractured his skull on the ceiling.

Of all the legendary crime families of the London underworld, The Driscoll Brothers are perhaps the least well known. For some villains, that would be an achievement – keep a low profile, get on with business and stay out of the limelight – and off the radar as far as the police are concerned. Had this have ever been their intention The Driscoll Brothers criminal empire could be deemed a huge success. But it wasn't really what they wanted at all. They wanted the notoriety. They wanted the kudos. They wanted to be feared as big-time gangsters. They never really got what they wanted. The most they succeeded in doing was ensuring that their name was feared throughout their manor.

They cast a giant shadow (well, one of them did) over Peckham where their intimidating presence was enough to ensure that most locals gave them a wide berth. Their greatest problem was that so did everyone else. Ever eager to demonstrate their own, and particularly brutal, brand of violence, rumour is that Ronnie Kray once told them to 'calm down a bit.' But according to some who knew the brothers, their low profile could have also been down to their low foreheads. As one old associate (who wishes to remain nameless) told this author: "There was once this guru who reckoned the world would end in a fortnight. Danny bet a grand that it would. And he was the brains of the outfit!"

Danny and Tony vanished in 2009 and are rumoured to be currently residing at the bottom of the Solent after accidently tangling with the Russian mafia. Their legendary status, however, has since rocketed, with reported sightings of the brothers in Rio, Papa New Guinea, the Himalayas, and even Chessington World of Adventures.

227

Peckham Echo

Thursday March 17th 2006

DRISCOLL BROTHERS WALK FREE

Local businessmen Danny and Tony Driscoll have been released on bail as their trial for human trafficking deteriorates into farce.

A recent photo of the Driscoll Brothers

All but one of the witnesses for the prosecution have withdrawn their testimonies and are refusing to give evidence. When asked why they thought this was happening, the Driscoll Brothers were mystified.

"We haven't a clue what's going on with these people," said Danny Driscoll. "First they were making up bizarre stories about us and now two of them have developed rampant amnesia."

"That's right," said his brother, Tony. "One of them can't remember his own name or where he lives and the other one just keeps saying 'Shredded Wheat' over and over again. Tragic."

The third witness has vanished completely. Local sources have named him as car salesman Aubrey Boyce who has sold his business and his house and disappeared with his family. The Driscoll Brothers deny any knowledge of Mr Boyce's whereabouts.

"Incredible, isn't it?" said Danny Driscoll. "We know Boycie really well. We've even had business dealings with him, video distribution as I recall. We really don't know where on earth he could be. But we'd like to."

en ... loves football, and he always comes in ... ge ... with my husband. ... ve ... we ... d ...

With The Compliments of

Danny & Tony Driscoll

GET WELL SOON

THE DRISCOLL BROTHERS HAVE BEEN KNOWN TO PREFER BLONDES!

Mickey and Jevon after a 'friendly warning' from the Driscolls!

Danny and Tony always knew how to make an enterance!

Peckham Echo

Thursday March 17th 2009

WHERE ARE THE DRISCOLL BROTHERS?

Local businessmen and alleged crime bosses Danny and Tony Driscoll have not been seen around their usual haunts in Peckham for months, prompting speculation that they have gone into hiding - but from whom?

One source in Peckham Market said: "Those two don't need to hide from nobody. If they ain't been seen it's because they don't want to be seen. They'll be back."

Sightings of the pair have been reported as far apart as Tahiti and Tescos in Southend. There are some however, who would be glad if they were never seen again.

Author Colin Wolf, who profiled the brothers in his book, Gangsters of London, said: "The less I say the better. After what I wrote about them in my book, they came round and nailed my nose to the bannister."

Peckham *Echo*

18 March 1985 • 18p

ST PATRICK'S DAY PUNCH-UP

Police were called to the Shamrock Club in Deptford last night when a massive brawl broke out while a new band from Peckham was playing.

The Shamrock Club is notorious for having had its alcohol and entertainment licences revoked due to disturbances on the premises but last night's fight was the biggest anyone can remember.

"It all started because of that poxy band they put on" said one regular. "We was promised songs by the Bachelors and Dana, and what we got was the biggest load of old crap east of Donegal."

The entertainers, Peckham-based A Bunch Of Wallies, fled from the scene apart from their lead singer, Michael Maguire who was caught up in the worst of the fighting.

"He couldn't sing for tuppence," said one regular, "but he could throw a mean right hook. And he has very sharp teeth."

Police made several arrests and are appealing for witnesses.

Continued Page 5

The budding stars rehearse!

Michael (Mental) Maguire

The band make a quick escape...

Mental Micky was happy enough fighting in the Shamrock!

SPORT: All the latest action from Peckham UTD's surprising local cup run from a special

BOYS WILL BE WALLIES

The charts saw a surprise assault at the end of the year from the band A Bunch Of Wallies with their hit *Boys Will Be Boys*. The band rocketed into the charts, enjoyed a brief spell in the limelight, and then dropped back into obscurity, so what happened to them?

Buch of Wallies frontman Mental Mickey Maguire dismisses the whole concept of fame. "We didn't want none of that," he says. "Being famous, having loads of dosh, being on telly, being driven around in Rollers, having birds ripping their kit off and wrapping themselves around you? I mean, who wants that? None of that really fitted with our philosophy as Marxist-Trotskyite-Anarchists."

Following a brief spell when their M-T-A philosophy evolved into a kind of angry-young-men- meet-post-new-romantic- punk phase, the members of the band have now all gone their separate ways, although Mental Mickey still knows where they all are. "I know where to get my hands on them if I ever want to," he says. "Stu works in a building society,

ABOVE: The band on *Top of the Pops*.

Charlie is a painter and decorator and our original drummer, Rodney, is still working on the market in Peckham. Not sure what happened to the replacement drummer, Whassisname, after he came out of hospital."

The hospitalisation of the drummer, Eric, heralded the break-up of the band. Is there any truth in the rumour that the break-up came about as the result of a brawl between the band members?

"I don't want to talk about that," says Mental Mickey. "Drummers are always a problem though, ain't they? Rodney kept trying to tell me what to do and so did that other bloke. I don't like people telling me what to do."

Might it be that the nickname Mental Mickey has something to do with the rumours of violence and Mickey attempting to bite people's ears off? "I don't like people calling me that," says Mental Mickey. "A couple of visits to Broadmoor and people think you're a head case, but I'm not, see? So don't say it!"

Maguire has branched out recently with his own fashion line, with designs that rely heavily on dagger-and-skull images and studded leather. Is this, too, a reflection of the old Mental Mickey violent image?

The interview was terminated at this point when Maguire screamed, "I told you not to call me that!" and leapt at the interviewer, attempting to gnaw his nose off. Mickey Maguire is now in police custody and can probably soon expect to be paying another of his occasional visits to Broadmoor. *RC*

A BUNCH OF WALLIES

Boys will be boys

A BUNCH OF WALLIES

s will be boys
(Sullivan)

1985 Peckham Records Ltd

A COLLECTOR'S ITEM!
THE BAND'S ONLY SINGLE!

FREDDIE ROBDAL
★ ★ ★ ★ ★ ★ ★ ★ ★ ★ ★ ★ ★ ★

FREDDIE THE FROG...
GENTLEMAN SAFECRACKER
AND BIG TIME CHARMER

PECKHAM 2½D ECHO

Monday, October 9, 1961

LOCAL MAN TO BE SENTENCED

LOCAL MAN Freddie Robdal is to be sentenced today for taking a public vehicle without the owner's permission, driving on the public highway without insurance and driving a vehicle without the appropriate licence. He was arrested last year whilst attending a party at one of the flats on the New World Estate, Peckham. He was then taken for questioning at the Peckham Police Station. New evidence became available which enabled the police to arrest the notorious thief. Detective Sergeant Thomas and Detective Constable Stanton were present at the arrest and have since been conducting the various interviews and enquiries. Robdal appeared to have been on the coach trip to Margate. However he admitted the offence to the court.

The incident happened last July when Robdal was with a group of regulars from the Nag's Head pub in Peckham on an outing to Margate.

Robdal and an associate known as 'Jelly Kelly' were previously arrested on suspicion of robbing a jeweller's in Margate but charges were dropped for lack of evidence.

Robdal admitted taking and driving away the vehicle, saying, "I realise it was wrong but thought it a bit of a lark at the time. I always wanted to be a bus driver." The vehicle was returned undamaged to the car park of a Margate pub where the rest of the group had stopped for refreshments. None of the rest of the group was aware that the incident had taken place.

The judge has warned that Robdal will be fined and that he will have his driving licence endorsed but said that he is unlikely to face a custodial sentence.

School Milk Off

THE MILK AT DOCKSIDE SECONDARY MODERN SCHOOL HAS BEEN CONTAMINATED WITH PETROL.

A former pupil at the school, Police Cadet Roy Slater, accompanied officers investigating what was feared might have been an attempt at mass poisoning. Cadet Slater said: "While the poisoning theory is obviously an issue, I personally believe that the milk was contaminated due to the urns and bottles having been used to transport petrol illegally.

"There are a number of youths in the area who ride around on mopeds and I suspect that they may have been able to get their hands on a quantity of fuel and then 'borrowed' the milk receptacles to transport the fuel."

"They then returned the milk receptacles and refilled them with milk without bothering to clean them out."

When asked if he knew who the culprits might be, Cadet Slater replied, "I know who they are all right. I might not be able to prove it, but I know. I'll get them all one day, you see if I don't!"

Innes Wins

Innes Ireland of Britain, driving a works Lotus, won the U.S. motor racing Grand Prix in New York yesterday at 103.22mph. Dan Surnet (U.S.) was second and Tony Brooks (Britain) was third.

Ireland took the lead at the Watkins Glen circuit when his Lotus team mate, Stirling Moss, developed engine trouble.

This is the first ever Grand Prix win for Ireland, although he has scored three victories in non-championship Formula One races.

Ireland's win is all the more remarkable in that it comes after he fought his way back to fitness following serious injuries sustained in a crash at Monaco in May.

H.M. Prison
DARTMOOR

Release Authorisation

This notification acts as proof of release from prison and that the term applied by the Court Service of Great Britain and Northern Ireland has been served in full or of a period applied post-sentence.

Name: .... FREDERICK ROBDAL ....

Prison Number: .... 7592001 ....

Release Date: .... THURSDAY FEBRUARY 4th 1960 ....

Governor: .... K.G.TINMOUTH ....

RITZ CINEMA ROBBED

The Ritz cinema was robbed last night by burglars who blew open the safe and escaped with around £2,000 in cash.

The thieves struck in the early hours of the morning after the manager, Mr Ernest Rayner, had locked up for the night.

"We are very security conscious here at the Ritz," said Mr Rayner. "I always double check that all of the exits and entrances are securely locked. I do have military training, you know, and I am relentlessly efficient in such matters."

Mr Rayner described a scene of devastation in his office. "The safe had been blown to pieces," he said, "and debris was scattered all over the desk. It has taken my temporary assistant manager, Mrs Trotter, all day to bring things back to some sort of order, but I fear she will have to spend a substantial amount of time in there with me to finish the job."

Police believe that the thieves had inside knowledge of the procedures at the cinema, staging their break-in at precisely the right moment. Takings from the whole week, including Saturday night, the busiest night of the week, are generally held in the safe until they can be banked on Monday morning. On a busy week, when a popular new movie is playing, the takings can amount to over £2,000.

Detective Sergeant Thomas of Peckham CID, said, "This was an inside job. Well, maybe not entirely an inside job because they did have to pick the locks on the emergency exit to get in and then blow the door off the safe instead of just opening it normally which they could have done if they had been able to unlock it which they would have been able to do if it was a real inside job.

"But they still had to know that there would be an entire week's takings in the safe, so somebody must have told them. Or maybe they just got lucky. Who knows? Stranger things have happened.

"We are following a number of leads and will pursue our enquiries vigorously to apprehend the perpetrators of this crime."

My darling Freddie,

You know me pretty well by now, I guess, and I know you, too. You once told me that we were very alike, and I know now that you was right. You have been right about so many things, Freddie.

You knew from the moment you first clapped eyes on me that I was the one for you, and you knew that I would feel the same way. You know ever such a lot about art, and antiques and you can even speak French. I love it when you speak French.

You've always said that we belong together, and you're right about that, too.

But it ain't going to happen, my darling. There's nothing I would like more than to turn my back on Reg and bring little Rodney to live with you in your cottage by the sea. But I can't leave Del behind, and Del will never leave Peckham behind. Left alone, Del and Reg would probably kill each other. Del still needs me, Freddie, and I can't leave him on his own.

Maybe one day, if Reg should tragically die slowly and horribly from some incredibly painful disease, I could be truly happy with you.

Until then, all I can do is hold you secretly in my heart and dream of a different life.

All my love,

Joan

FREDDIE MADE MUM'S LIFE THE EXCITING ADVENTURE SHE ALWAYS CRAVED

OPEN VISIT ORDER

*I/We wish to visit:

F. ROBDAL

| Registered number | 44789C | location | WS |

	VISITOR(S)	INMATE
*Mr./Mrs./Miss	IRENE TURPIN	FREDERICK ROBDAL
No. & street	41, ORCHARD STREET	
District	PECKHAM	
Town & postal code	LONDON SE26	
Tel. number (if any)	-	
Signature	T.Turpin	

VISIT

| Began | 2.30pm | Ended | | Date | 23.10.61 |

| Visitor's signature | I.Turpin | | Signature of Officer supervising visit |

*To be completed by visitor(s) before handing form to officer supervising visit

GOLD BULLION STILL MISSING

Police have made at least four arrests following the raid on Stratton's Merchant Bank and Bullion Depository but £250,000 of stolen gold is still missing.

Inspector McMorse of Scotland Yard said: "We believe that there is at least one other member of this gang who is still at large. If we can find him, we will find the gold."

The raid took place last month at dead of night and the robbers were able to enter the premises undetected before cracking the combination lock on the gold vault and making off with an unknown number of gold bars.

"The gold must have weighed quite a bit," said Inspector McMorse, "so it would not have been easy to carry. Anyone who has any information about this crime should contact me at Scotland Yard."

Inspector McMorse also warned that the gang member who is on the run might well be armed, is most certainly a desperate, dangerous individual and should not be approached by members of the public.

St Mary's Parish Church
Seaview Road
Clifton
Hampshire

Mr F Robdal
Spinacre Cottage
Clifton
Hampshire

12 September 1963

Dear Mr Robdal

I am writing to thank you for your most generous donation of
the stained glass windows that have so transformed our little
church. As you know from the many times you spent in quiet
contemplation in the church, St Mary's has always been an
oasis of peace and tranquility. The windows have only served
to enhance that atmosphere and they will be appreciated by the
congregation, dwindling though it may be, for years to come.

I do hope that you were pleased with the service at which I
officiated for your dear friend Alfred Broderick. I am sorry
that I couldn't be there for the moment that his coffin was
actually committed to the deep but, as you said, it was rather
a small boat and rather a large coffin. Mr Broderick must
indeed have been a 'larger than life' character as it took
eight of us to carry the coffin down to the boat. You must
have been very fond of him and I will never forget you saying
in your eulogy that he had 'not just a heart of gold, he was
solid gold.' Very touching.

Please feel free to drop in to St Mary's whenever your are
passing. Our door is always open, spiritually speaking.
We do now tend to lock up at night as there are some very
disreputable characters around these days.

Yours faithfully

Rev Ian Sturrock

Reverend Ian Sturrock

REV STURROCK PICTURED IN 1963

PECKHAM ECHO

2½D

Sunday 27th August 1963

LOCAL VILLAINS DIE IN BLAST

Robdal and Kelly pictured when they were arrested in 1960

Two notorious local thieves have died while attempting to rob a post office in Plumstead.

Freddie Robdal and his accomplice Gerald 'Jelly' Kelly had broken into the post office and were in the process of blowing the safe when both were killed in a premature explosion.

The incident happened around 2.00 am in the morning on Tuesday and witnesses claim that the blast could be heard as far afield as Woolwich.

"I wondered what the hell was going on," said one man. "One second I was sound asleep and the next the missus was running round the room screaming that the Blitz was back. She had a doodlebug land on her auntie's house."

Police and fire brigade investigators have been sifting through the rubble in order to piece together exactly what happened.

"It seems that the thieves entered the premises by forcing a window at the back," said a police spokesman. "They then proceeded to the strongroom where the safe was. Kelly was preparing the gelignite to blow the safe when it appears that Robdal sat on the detonator."

Robdal's body was found by firemen on the roof of the building on the opposite side of the street. "It was a bizarre sight," said Leading Fireman Sam Taylor. "He looked just like he had been sitting there having a laugh. There was hardly a mark on him and he was propped against a chimney breast, crouched like he was sitting, smiling and still holding a little slim cigar. It had gone out."

Police were quick to quash any rumours that Kelly may have made

his escape after the blast. "We believe Kelly died at the scene," said the police spokesman.

When pressed about why he didn't think Kelly could be on the run, the spokesman replied, "It is extremely unlikely that he is on the run. We believe he was holding the explosives when Robdal sat on the detonator. All we found of Kelly were his shoes, and his feet were still in them. It's not easy to go on the run with no feet."

It is believed that Robdal and Kelly served together in the Royal Navy as sabotage and demolition experts but turned to a life of crime after the war. They are alleged to have been involved in a number of robberies across the south of England where explosives were used to break into safes.

STRANGERS LURKING IN GRAVEYARD

Police were called to St Mary's Church in Clifton when dog walkers spotted three men lurking in the graveyard with a shovel.

"We thought that they were up to no good," said Mrs Barbara Jones of Smugger's Close in Clifton. "There was a tall, skinny one, a small dark-haired one, and a very old man with a huge white beard. At one point the little one looked like he was going to whack the old man on the head with the shovel."

When police officers arrived, the elderly gentleman claimed that they were out looking for buried gold, but the others denied this, saying that they were actually just thinking

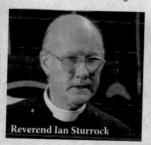

Reverend Ian Sturrock

about building a sandcastle on the beach.

The vicar at St Mary's, Reverend Ian Sturrock, said that one of the men had donated a computer to the church. "They were actually very decent people," said Reverend Sturrock. "They do have a historic connection to the church as the stained glass windows were donated by a friend or relative and the niece of another friend was recently married here."

Reverend Sturrock was especially pleased when one of the men donated a brand new computer to the church.

"I'm not sure we really need a computer," he said, "and I don't know how these things work - or even IF this one works - but if anyone would like to take it off our hands, I can let you have it at a knock-down price."

St Mary's Church in Clifton

Two of the lurking men

The moment we knew where the Frog's gold was...

Our family legacy just a few miles out at sea!

DANGER DOLLS

★ ★ ★ ★ ★ ★ ★ ★ ★ ★

Lusty Linda, Erotic Estelle
& FRIENDS...

Self-inflating, deluxe blow up dolls for the more discerning weirdo who wants to get it on with half a pound of latex and a lump of oxygen!!

From This: To This:

£60

ALBERT HAD AN INFLATED OPINION OF HIS CHAT-UP LINES!

Does Cassandra let you do that to her Rodders?

Mum's old clothes really came in handy!

Nothing worse than back-seat drivers!

Peckham *Echo*

17 January 1989 • 18p

DEADLY DOLLS
DESTROY DEPTFORD FACTORY

A consignment of inflatable dolls is thought to have been responsible for the destruction of a plastics factory in Deptford, causing over £1 million of damage.

The fiery aftermath at the Deptford factory

Deptford Mouldings produced tools, toys and garden furniture but one range manufactured on the premises, a type of inflatable doll, caused a fire that gutted the factory. The dolls used an inflation device that should have pumped compressed air into the dolls but had been fitted with canisters of highly inflammable propane by mistake.

The Fire Brigade were naturally cautious in dealing with the blaze. "Once we realised that there were tanks of propane on the premises, as well as all of the other chemicals used in plastic mouldings, we had to play it safe," said Chief Fire Officer Sam Pendleton. "We did our best to contain the blaze, having made sure there was nobody in the building. So we were shocked when we saw a naked body shoot out through an upstairs window and explode like a giant firework. Bits of burning flesh came raining down, but they turned out to be plastic. It was one of those dolls."

Most of the stock of dolls, as well as everything else, is thought to have been destroyed in the fire, but it is believed that up to 50 of the deadly dolls are unaccounted for. A security guard spotted what is suspected to be a falsified signature on a delivery note, meaning that the rogue dolls are still on the loose somewhere in South East London.

Members of the public are warned to leave these dolls well alone. They were intended for the adult entertainment market and can be identified by their names, such as Lusty Linda and Erotic Estelle.

Barry Hodges, proprietor of the Ecstasy shop in Peckham, says he knows nothing about the dolls. "I would be very suspicious if anyone were to come to my back door offering me something like this in the middle of the night," he said. "Even if it was someone that I had known for years and who previously sold me a gross of reject genuine Metropolitan Police handcuffs that had been accidentally dyed pink."

"I ain't even in business any more anyway," said Mr Hodges. "The council shut me down last week. Tell you what, though, anybody who does have some fun with one of them things best not light a fag afterwards. There's a bang with a difference, innit?"

Police could neither confirm nor deny reports of unexplained late-night explosions on Peckham Rye Common and whether these could be linked to the discovery of unidentifiable scraps of charred pink plastic.

(Dirty) Barry Hodges

A NASTY SELFISH EXCUSE
FOR A FATHER - REG TROTTER

Form FF1457

London Borough of Peckham
Council Housing Tenancy Application Form

Your details

Surname _Trotter_

Christian name(s) _Reginald_

Current address _39 Orchard Street_
Peckham
London

Date of birth _26/6/20_ | Place of birth _Bermondsey_

Marital status _Married_ | Date of marriage _1944_

Type of building _Terrace_

Full name of spouse _Joan Mavis Trotter_

Type of occupancy _Rented_

D.O.B. of spouse _10/7/24_ | Place of birth _Clapham_

Period of occupancy _30 years_

Children's names and ages _Derek Trotter 16._

Previous addresses in the last five years (please include details of type and period of occupancy and reason for ending tenancy)

Current employment _Laborer_

Employed since _Unemployed_

Employer's name and address

Military service details, if any
Unfit for military service

OUR FIRST HOME ON ORCHARD STREET

Accommodation

Preferred type of accommodation _Nice modern glamorous_

Preferred location of accommodation _California Peckham_

Number of people who will live with you and their relationship to you
Four. The missus, baby on the way, invalid father, teenage son

Reason for preferred location (e.g. work/schools)
My wife has two jobs locally, at The Ritz and as a part-time filing clerk with the council

Acceptable locations _Peckham, New World Estate_

Minimum requirements from accommodation _New, clean, nice, airy, high-rise block, inside bog_

Acceptable types of accommodation _New flat in with all mod cons in a high-rise block_

Signature _Reginald Trotter_

Date _Date - 25th June 1960_

NATIONAL SERVICE (ARMED FORCES) ACT, 1939

ENLISTMENT NOTICE

YOU SHOULD TAKE
THIS NOTICE
WITH YOU WHEN
YOU REPORT.

MINISTRY OF LABOUR AND NATIONAL SERVICE
EMPLOYMENT EXCHANGE,
EXCHANGE HOUSE,
CARLTON ROAD,
PECKHAM, LONDON SE15.

Date *31 October 1940*

Mr. *Reginald Trotter*

39 Orchard Street

Peckham

Registration No. *166854*

DEAR SIR,

In accordance with the National Service (Armed Forces) Act, 1939, you are called

upon for service in the ....TERRITORIAL ARMY.......... and are required to present yourself

on *10* day *November* 19*40*, at 10 a.m., or as early

as possible thereafter on that day, to :—

Exchange House

Carlton Road

Peckham Rye (nearest railway station).

Delete
if not
applic-
able

A Travelling Warrant for your journey is enclosed. Before starting your journey you must exchange the warrant for a ticket at the booking office named on the warrant. If possible, this should be done a day or two before you are due to travel.

A Postal Order for 4s. in respect of advance of service pay, is also enclosed. Uniform and personal kit will be issued to you after joining H.M. Forces. Any kit that you take with you should not exceed an overcoat, change of clothes, stout pair of boots, and personal kit, such as razor, hair brush, tooth brush, soap and towel.

Immediately on receipt of this notice, you should inform your employer of the date upon which you are required to report for service.

Yours faithfully,

W. FRASER

N.S. 12   (4884) Wt. 27800—8813 9/39 B.W. 677

39 Orchard Street
Peckham
London SE15

W. Fraser
Divisional Controller
Ministry of Labour and National Service
Labour Exchange
Exchange House
Carlton Road
Peckham
London SE15

Dear Mr Fraser

There seems to have been an orrible mistake regarding the call-up papers what was sent to my son, Reginald. Like me, Reg suffers somethin awful from back pains, a dodgy belly, colour blindness, a weak chest, arthritis, hammer toes, breathlessness, twitchin eyelids and unusual pimples on the soles of his feet. He can't hear much, either, just like me. We're as deaf as two bricks.

Reg is, as an actual matter of fact, struggling terribly with his back today. He just can't get it out of bed. His mother had to take him in a spot of breakfast before she went off to work and I'm hopin' that she'll be poppin back at lunchtime to make us a sandwich as my belly thinks me throat's been cut. Anyway, because Reg is so poorly, I am writing you this here letter to say that he won't be comin to join the army.

A few months back, our doctor signed papers excusing us from any kind of military service, and most kinds of work, so I don't think you need to bother tryin to call up young Reg again any time soon.

Yours
Edward Trotter

REG TROTTER:
NO GOOD WASTER

MUM AND GRANDAD OFTEN DESPAIRED
AT WHAT THE ROTTEN SOD GOT UP TO

39 Orchard Street
Peckham
London SE15

The Clerk of the Court
Southwark Crown Court
Wilmot Drive
Southwark
London SE10

Dear Sir

I am afraid that I am unable to attend for
Jury Service on the date that you said in your
Jury Summons as I have recently taken Holy Orders
as a novice monk in the newly formed Divine Order
of Peckham Brotherhood.

As such, my religious status excludes me from having
to sit on a jury.

Yours sincerely

Brother Reg Trotter

DAD ALWAYS HAD A BARMAID
ON THE GO...

NEWCASTLE GENERAL INFIRMARY
Tyneview Street, Newcastle upon Tyne

Reginald Trotter
127 Nelson Mandela House
New World Estate
Peckham
London SE15

Dear Mr Trotter

As it has proved to be impossible to locate you at any address we
have tried in the North East, I am sending this letter to the last
known address listed for you in London.

You have been absent from work now for almost seven months and we
have long since assumed that you have no intention of returning to
Newcastle to face a disciplinary hearing at the hospital. Basically,
had you not already disappeared, we would have formally terminated
your employment as a porter here. Criminal charges may also have
been brought against you.

Allegations were made, with abundant evidence to back them up,
that on several occasions your activities were detrimental to the
wellbeing of the patients.

Selling alcohol on Ward 7 'to cheer up the miserable gits', as you
put it, could have had serious consequences for these patients as
they are all on courses of medication to combat clinical depression.
Fortunately, you had watered down the alcohol to increase your
profits so the only real problem was the disturbance to patients in
neighbouring wards from the singing and dancing.

There were also many complaints from patients and their relatives
about you 'running a book' to take bets on 'who's gonna pop their
clogs next' on the geriatric ward and 'who's gonna pop one out next'
on the paediatric ward. We have never before been in a situation
where patients were asking relatives to bring cash at visiting time
to cover their gambling debts.

There were also charges of sleeping on duty, making inappropriate
remarks to nursing staff and abusing hospital equipment by hooking
yourself up to a patient's saline drip in order to rehydrate yourself
when you had a hangover.

Should you ever read this letter, Mr Trotter, please let me make it
clear that we are taking steps to ensure that you are never employed in
any position of trust in any hospital anywhere in Britain ever again.

Yours sincerely

Theresa Goodbody

Theresa Goodbody
Hospital Administrator

AFTER WALKING OUT 18 YEARS EARLIER
THE GHOST OF CHRISTMAS PAST RETURNED IN 1983

LOT 73
THE HARRISON H6 'LESSER WATCH'

John Harrison was a talented clock and watchmaker, almost entirely self-taught, who invented a type of marine chronometer that solved the problem of accurately executing the complex calculations required to establish longitude at sea. This was a problem of such magnitude that the British Government offered a £20,000 prize to whomever could find a solution - equivalent to almost £3 million today.

This huge advance in marine navigation made Harrison one of the most famous watchmakers of the 18th century.

Born in Yorkshire in 1693, Harrison followed his father into the family carpentry business but also displayed a talent for understanding the workings of clocks, which he took to repairing in his spare time. It is said that his lifelong fascination with watches began when he was given a watch to amuse himself as he lay in bed at the age of six, suffering with a bout of smallpox. The young Harrison took the watch apart, rebuilt it and came to comprehend the mechanics of clocks, appreciating precisely how a watch should be designed to make it as accurate as possible.

By the age of 20, Harrison had built his own clock, designing it himself from scratch and hand-crafting all of the moving parts from wood. Some of these early wooden clocks survive to this day and are displayed from time to time at museums and galleries, mainly in London.

Harrison soon graduated to manufacturing his timepieces from brass and other metals, with jewelled movements and incredibly intricate, most beautiful and inventive engineering. Harrison made six watches to the standard of his marine chronometers. Four are known to be in the possession of the National Maritime Museum in Greenwich. One is held by the Worshipful Company of Clockmakers in London.

The watch offered for sale is the sixth in the series, the Harrison H6. Design drawings for this watch have been held at the National Maritime Museum for a number of years, but the watch itself went missing over 250 years ago and its whereabouts have been unknown - until now.

Peckham antiques dealers Trotters Independent Traders unearthed the watch recently amongst a large collection of other valuables and immediately realised the importance of their find.

This is a rare opportunity to acquire a historic piece and bidding is expected to reflect its importance.

FOR 15 YEARS THAT LITTLE WATCH HAD BEEN LYING ABOUT THE GARAGE!

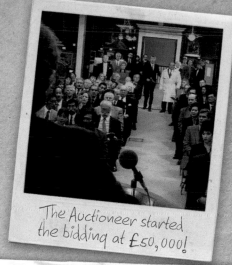

The Auctioneer started the bidding at £50,000!

My 'Midwife on emergency call' sign came in handy!

All those numbers... It all got too much!

SOTHEBY'S
Founded 1774

Sotheby's Auction House's London,
New Bond Street, Sussex,
London, Olympia

Ref: TR/56384/02

RECEIPT OF SALE

Harrison, John

Session - 1 47578
Date of Auction : 23/6
Auctioneer   T Cuthbertson
Lot Number   (73 of 162)

Mr Derek Trotter & Mr Rodney Trotter
127 Nelson Mandela House
Peckham
London

Auction of Lot 73

John Harrison - H6 Solid Silver Pocket Marine Time Keeper

Lot No.	Reserve	Starting Bid	Reserve not met	Final Bid	Final Bid
73	150,000.00	-	-	6.2 Million	

TERMS

A formal evaluation of the fair market and/or insurance value of a given piece or group of property. Fair market value represents what we believe an item would bring at auction. Insurance value reflects what we believe it would cost to replace an item. Since an appraisal is made by comparing the object at hand with similar works that sold recently, an appraiser must know the market well. No appraisal is definitive.

Sotheby's Auctioneers & Valuers
Founded 1744

Business & Finance

March 2001

RAGS TO RICHES TO RAGS

In our exclusive interview Trotter Independent Traders give their illuminating story

One moment we were living the high life...

...then we realised it was time to leg it!

RAGS **TO** RICHES **TO** RAGS

The collapse of the Central American Stock Market took investors by surprise all over the world and the economic ripples from this major catastrophe will be felt for years to come.

One company that can best illustrate the impact that the crash had on small businesses is Trotters Independent Traders, a family-run enterprise which, according to company founder Derek Trotter, dealt in imports and exports, mainly concentrating on "electrical goods, luxury goods and antiques." The company's entire investment portfolio was tied to the CASM and when the market folded, all of the companies assets were lost, leaving behind substantial tax liabilities, meaning that they were facing mounting debts for the first time in years. What were Mr Trotter's thoughts when he first heard about the CASM crash?

"Well," said Derek, "my first thought was 'Menage a trois!' You see, in my many years of dealing with foreigners, I have not only picked up a bit of the lingo, but I have found that when you are surrounded by the locals, you start to think in their language and act like them, too.

"My younger brother is much the same. I remember taking him to the monkey house at the zoo when he was a nipper. I only turned my back for a second, to give directions to a charming Dutch mademoiselle, and when I looked back he was sitting on top of his pram eating a banana and slinging the contents of his nappy at passers by.

"He still enjoys doing that. Eating a banana, that, is, not slinging the …. Anyway, we had

Above: Derek Trotter and his significant other Raquel outside their former family home.

to leg it back to London sharpish to have a conflab with our broker and our accountant. Unfortunately, they had both discovered an urgent need to be in Acapulco and we ain't seen neither of them since. That was it - we lost the lot. Everything we owned."

Returning to London meant that Derek and his family had to face up to the fact that the lifestyle they had enjoyed when their investments were growing and providing a very healthy return had to change substantially. How did they cope in their new circumstances?

"The Trotters are a 'never say die' sort of family," said Derek. "He Who Dares Wins has always been our motto and we knew that we had to pick ourselves up and get stuck in to a bit of business again.

"Fortunately, one of the few things that hadn't been registered for tax purposes as a company asset was our London apartment. It made sense to move in and use that as our base of operations. The TITco warehouse is also very close by. Having taken full responsibility for our losses, even though it was the broker and the accountant what landed us right in it (and if I ever catch up with them they can both expect a right swift kick up the jacksy), I had to step down as Managing Director. Taking more of a back office, advisory role was difficult for me at first as I was used to being integral to the running of the company - the mynchpin, so to speak.

"My brother, Rodney, took on a lot of that responsibility and, as time goes by, my son, Damien will play a bigger part in our operations. The Trotters are definitely on the up-and-up again. This time next year, we'll be millionaires … again."

Above: A proud day - with the Queen and Prince Philip at the opening of the Trotter Wing.

Words: Olivia Hubbard

£3,000 REWARD FOR RARE BUTTERFLY

In the summer months, visitors flock to our shores, despite the famously unreliable nature of Britiain's weather. The weather doesn't appear to deter the tourists, but there has been one surprise visitor this year that is usually only seen in far sunnier climes.

The Jamaican Swallowtail butterfly (papilus humorous) normally enjoys warm sunny days in the Caribbean, but a handful of them make their way to Europe, carried by warm trans-atlantic air currents, during the summer.

The butterflies normally restrict themselves to southern Europe and the Mediterranean, but several have been spotted this year in the south of England. Butterfly fanciers have seen this extremely rare type in Kent and even close to London in Greenwich Park.

"This is a very rare species even in its native Caribbean home," said entymologist and butterfly enthusiast Dr Harold Crippen of the British Buttefrly Conservationists (BBC). "For there to be even one sighting in England is enormously exciting, but this year there have been several reports."

The beautiful colouring and markings of this rare breed mean that it has become

The Jamaican Swallowtail butterfly (papilus humorous)

something of a 'Holy Grail' for butterfly fanciers who count it as one of their 'must see' species.

"The Jamaican Swallowtail is, in fact, an endangered species," said Dr Crippen. "There are plans to instigate a breeding programme for captive examples in order to increase their numbers. First, of course, we would have to capture live specimens.

"These creatures are very shy and very elusive, but for the capture of a live specimen, the BBC would be willing to offer a reward of £3,000."

So, if you are out and about in Kent or the parks of East London this summer, take your butterfly net with you and keep your eyes peeled for the Jamaican Swallowtail - you could be £3,000 richer!

Be careful, take yer time... that thing is worth £3000!

Nice 'n' easy Rodney almost there!

Excerpts from John Sullivan's personal scripts and notes

1989-2003

THE SENDING OF THIS SCRIPT DOES NOT CONSTITUTE AN OFFER OF A CONTRACT FOR ANY PART IN IT.

BBC TELEVISION

LIGHT ENTERTAINMENT (COMEDY) — REHEARSAL SCRIPT

3 5 6 7 8 9 11 12 13 15 19 21 22 23 24

"ONLY FOOLS AND HORSES" Series 'F'

by

JOHN SULLIVAN

"CHAIN GANG"

Episode 4.

Producer .... GARETH GWENLAN
Director .... TONY DOW
Production Manager .... ADRIAN PEGG
Production Assistant .... AMITA LOCHAB
Assistant Floor Manager .... KERRY WADDELL

* *

Programme No:	1/LLC K754E
Production Office:	Room 7022 TV Centre Tel. 01-743-8000 Ext. 2153/1558 DL: 01-576-1558

* *

Filming:	7th November-2nd December 1988
Studio Recording:	Saturday 14th & Sunday 15th January 1988
TX DATE:	SUNDAY 22ND JANUARY 1989

SCENE 2. INT. THE ONE ELEVEN

CLUB. NIGHT. STUDIO

*All similarities to the
Richardsons 'Two Eleven Club' are
purely coincidental*

UNLIKE MONTE CARLO THE EMPHASIS
HERE IS ON CARD GAMES AND ONE-
ARMED BANDITS AS OPPOSED TO
ROULETTE. ALSO THE ONLY PEOPLE
WEARING EVENING SUITS (SAVE FOR
DEL) ARE THE BOUNCERS WHO ALL
LOOK AS IF THEY HAVE JUST
FINISHED GOVERNMENT TRAINING
SCHEMES TO BECOME JURY-NOBBLERS.

THE CLIENTELE IS VARIED IN AGE
AND STYLE. WE HAVE THE OBVIOUS
HEAVIES IN THEIR TWO AND THREE
PIECE TRADITIONAL SUITS - THE
SLIGHTLY YOUNGER SET WITH THEIR
GLENN HODDLE HAIRCUTS AND 'MADE
FOR SOMEONE MUCH BIGGER THAN ME'
CLOTHES AND A STRONG CONTINGENT
FROM THE 'GREENPEACE' SECTION OF
THE YARDIES. THE WOMEN REFLECT
THEIR MENS' TASTES WHICH ARE
USUALLY HOT AND SPICY AND COME IN
TIN FOIL CONTAINERS. THERE ARE
MORE BREASTS AND THIGHS ON SHOW
THAN ON SAINSBURY'S POULTRY
COUNTER.

THE DECOR IS TRADITIONAL RE-PRO:
CHANDELIERS, CRYSTAL-EFFECT TABLE
LAMPS, ETC.

THE FURNISHINGS ARE SIMILAR; RE-
PRO GEORGIAN CHAIRS, A CHAISE
LONGUE OR TWO.

ALL IN ALL IT SHOULD LOOK LIKE
BARBARA CARTLAND'S WEDDING LIST.

AS WITH ANY LICENCED GAMING
PREMISES THE MEMBERS PLAY WITH
PLASTIC CHIPS.
WE HAVE THE LARGE MAIN 'PLAYING
AREA' (OF WHICH WE WILL SEE
LITTLE - JUST A GLIMPSE OF A CARD
GAME OR WHATEVER IS NECESSARY TO
GIVE THE ATMOSPHERE OF A GAMING
CLUB).

2

WE ALSO USE THE BAR (WHICH WE
SHALL BE CONCENTRATING ON) AND
THE ENTRANCE FOYER.

WE COME ON CARD TABLE WHERE DEL
IS SITTING. HE IS WEARING HIS
EVENING SUIT AND SATIN BOW TIE.

DURING HIS CONVERSATION WITH
TRIGGER, THE CROUPIER DEALS HIM
TWO CARDS.

TRIGGER APPROACHES. HE WEARS HIS
'BEST CLOTHES' COMPLETE WITH THE
VIVID V NECK (AS PER CHRISTMAS
SPECIAL). HE SITS NEXT TO DEL.

TRIGGER:
Alright, Del-Boy?

DEL:
Wotchyer, Trigger.

TRIGGER:
No Dave?

DEL:
Yeah he's coming down later,

bringing that bird of his,

Cassandra.

TRIGGER:
He's getting a bit serious, ain

he?

DEL:
As serious as that little plonker

can ever be. (DEL NOTICES

SOMEONE STANDING AT BAR) That

bloke at the bar.

3

LET US SEE <u>ARNIE</u> STANDING AT BAR
LAUGHING AND JOKING WITH BARMAN.

ARNIE IS IN HIS LATE, LATE
FORTIES.

HE IS SMARTLY DRESSED AND, WE
SHALL DISCOVER, SPEAKS WITH A
MIDDLE-OF-THE-ROAD ACCENT - IT'S
NEITHER REFINED NOR ROUGH - IT'S
THE KIND OF ACCENT THE MANAGER OF
YOUR LOCAL B & Q WOULD HAVE.
ARNIE IS A FRIENDLY AND GENUINE
KIND OF PERSON ("A SOLID BLOKE").
HE HAS A GENTLE AND GENEROUS
NATURE AND SEEMS RELAXED AND AT
ONE WITH THE WORLD. HE HAS AN
ENDLESS STORE OF JOKES AND AN
EVER READY AND SINCERE LAUGH.
HE'S THE KIND OF BLOKE THAT
ANYONE WOULD GET ALONG WITH AND
<u>TRUST</u>.

<u>TRIGGER:</u>
Who Arnie?

<u>DEL:</u>
Yeah Arnie. D'you know much

about him?

<u>TRIGGER:</u>
Not a lot. He only moved to the

area a few weeks agc. Seems a

nice bloke though. He's a

retired jewellery dealer, ain he?

<u>DEL:</u>
Yeah that's what he told me.

Retired early ain he?

<u>TRIGGER:</u>
Maybe he made enough, Del. You

lining something up then?

4

DEL:
Dunno, Trig. I've bin having a
few chats and drinks with him
over the last couple of weeks.
He let it slip that, even though
he's retired, he still does a bit
of 'Private' business. All cash
and confidential, keep the old
tax man off his back. I thought
I might give him a shove, see
what I can pick up.

TRIGGER:
I heard your firm was broke.

DEL:
I'm a businessman, Trigger, I
always keep a bit pugged away for
emergencies. Anyway, who told
you we was broke?

TRIGGER:
Dave.

DEL:
Take no notice of him, he's only
my financial director, what does
he know about it! (REFERRING TO
HIS TWO CARDS) Look at this.
I'm doing alright here.

5

TRIGGER:
(HAS ALSO BEEN DEALT TWO CARDS)

D'you want these? I'm not

playing.

DEL:
Bloody 'ell, Trig! Take 'em with

you, you'll ruin the game.

TRIG EXITS.

DEL:
(CONT) (TO CROUPIER. HE MEANS

GIVE ME ANOTHER CARD)

Go'n.

THE CROUPIER DEALS HIM ANOTHER
CARD.

ARNIE APPEARS NEXT TO HIM.

ARNIE:
How you doing?

DEL:
Wotchyer, Arnie. I didn't spot

you.

ARNIE:
I've only been here five minutes,

most of that was spent arguing

with that doorman, Otto, or

whatever he's called.

6

(COMPLETE)

THE SENDING OF THIS SCRIPT DOWS NOT CONSTITUTE AND OFFER OF A
CONTRACT FOR ANY PART OF IT

<u>BBC TELEVISION</u>   <u>REHEARSAL SCRIPT</u>

<u>LIGHT ENTERAINMENT (COMEDY)</u>

<u>"ONLY FOOLS & HORSES"</u>   <u>CHRISTMAS SPECIAL 1989</u>

by

<u>JOHN SULLIVAN</u>

<u>"The Jolly Boys' Outing"</u>

Producer .... GARETH GWENLAN
Director .... TONY DOW
Production Manager .... ADRIAN PEGG
Production Assistant .... AMITA LOCHAB
Assistant Floor Manager .... ANGIE DE CHASTELAI SMITH

* *

Programme No: 50/LLC A090A

Production Office: Room 7022 TV Centre
                      Tel. 01-743-8000   Ext. 2153/1558
                      DL: 01-576-1558

* *

Filming: 1st-22nd May 1989

Studio Recording: Wednesday 3rd May 1989
                      Friday 2nd-Sunday 4th June 1989

SCENE 10. EXT. MARGATE.

DAY. FILM.

THEY ARRIVE IN
MARGATE.

(INC. HELICOPTER SHOT)

THEN MONTAGE TO MUSIC
OF A DAY IN MARGATE.

93

SCENE 11. EXT. BEACH. DAY. FILM.

THE MUSIC 'EVERYBODY'S
TALKING AT ME' FADES
AND WE FIND DEL AND
RODNEY LAYING ON BEACH
OR SITTING ON WALL OR
WHATEVER.

IT IS NOW SIX IN THE
EVENING AND THEY ARE
BOTH LOOKING TIRED AND
RAGGED.

RODNEY:
Well, our coach leaves in an hour.

Not been a bad day though, has it?

DEL:
No, it's bin alright, bruv, enjoyed

meself ... I'm cream-crackered. I

think I might have yuppy-flu.

RODNEY:
Yeah? Couldn't have anything to do

with the lobster vindaloo and

fourteen pina coladas, could it?

94

DEL:
Well, I s'ppose that might have slowed me down a bit ... I went down the cemetery yesterday - took some flowers for Mum.

RODNEY:
(EMBARRASSED) I ain't bin down there lately, Del - there's always something to do.

DEL:
Mum understands, Rodders. She knows you think about her.

RODNEY:
Yeah, I do.

DEL:
I just sat there and told her what's bin happening ... I bet she was well pleased. Cassandra reminds me of Mum, you know.

RODNEY:
(AT FIRST HE HAS A WORRIED EXPRESSION AS HE THINKS OF MUM'S REPUTATION) Oh - good.

95

7th Serie

THE SENDING OF THIS SCRIPT DOES NOT CONSTITUTE AN OFFER OF A
CONTRACT FOR ANY PART IN IT

<u>BBC TELEVISION</u>   <u>REHEARSAL SCRIPT</u>

<u>LIGHT ENTERTAINMENT (COMEDY)</u>   (2nd Draft 20.11.92)

"ONLY FOOLS & HORSES"   CHRISTMAS SPECIAL 1992

'Mother Nature's Son'

by

JOHN SULLIVAN

```
Director ................................ TONY DOW
Producer ................................ GARETH GWENLAN
Executive Producer ..................... JOHN SULLIVAN
Production Manager ..................... SUE LONGSTAFF
Production Assistant ................... AMITA LOCHAB
Assistant Floor Manager ................ JENNY PENROSE
```

****

Programme No: 1/LLC D745N

Production Office: Room 4109 Television Centre

Direct Line: 081-576-7705

Tel: 081-743-8000   Ext. 3704/3710/7705

Fax: 081-743-2457

****

Filming: Tuesday 24th November-Monday 7th December 1992

Studio Recording: Saturday 19th & Sunday 20th December 1992

<u>TX DATE:</u>   <u>FRIDAY 25TH DECEMBER 1992, time tba</u>

WHEN THIS SCENE WENT
BEFORE CAMERAS
THIS DREAM SEQUENCE WAS
MOVED TO THE NAGS HEAD

FROM OPENING TITLES AND MUSIC

WE MIX THROUGH TO:

SCENE 1. INT. TROTTERS LOUNGE.

STUDIO. NIGHT

THIS, AS WE SHALL SOON
DISCOVER, IS A DREAM SEQUENCE,
ALTHOUGH THE AUDIENCE SHOULD
NOT BE AWARE OF THIS.

THE GREATEST PARTY IN THE
WORLD IS TAKING PLACE IN THE
TROTTERS FLAT (COULD EVEN BE A
CHRISTMAS PARTY - CHRISTMAS
TREE, CARDS, DECORATIONS,
ETC). EVERYONE IS THERE.
"MERRY CHRISTMAS" BY SLADE IS
PLAYING LOUDLY. ALTHOUGH
EVERYONE WILL BE AD-LIBBING
THE MUSIC SHOULD BE OVER THE
TOP LOUD AND WE NEVER QUITE
HEAR WHAT ANYONE IS SAYING.

THERE IS SO MUCH FOOD, SO MUCH
BOOZE, SO MUCH FUN, SO MUCH
LOVE THAT EVERYONE IN THE
COUNTRY SHOULD WISH THEY WERE
AT THIS WONDERFUL PARTY.

EVERYONE IS SMILING, YOU CAN
HARDLY SEE WHAT'S HAPPENING
FOR GLINTING HAMPSTEADS.

WITHOUT COMMENTING ON IT TOO
MUCH SOME PEOPLE ARE BEHAVING
UNCHARACTERISTICALLY. BOYCIE
AND MARLENE ARE JIVING, ROD
AND CASSANDRA ARE DOING A
SMOOCH AND KISSING QUITE
PASSIONATELY.

1

AT THIS POINT RAQUEL IS
HOLDING THE TWENTY TWO MONTH
OLD DAMIEN WHO WEARS A T SHIRT
WITH HIS NAME EMBLAZONED
ACROSS THE FRONT (JUST IN CASE
ANY OF THE AUDIENCE HAVE NOT
SEEN THE LAST SERIES).

DAMIEN HOLDS A HELIUM INFLATED
BALLOON.

WITH HAND-HELD CAMERA WE
MINGLE THROUGH THE HAPPY
CROWD.

A HAPPY RAQUEL HANDS THE BABY
TO DEL WHILST SHE REFILLS HER
GLASS WITH CHAMPAGNE.

DEL DANCES WITH DAMIEN FOR
AWHILE UNTIL, SURPRISINGLY,
RODNEY OPENS HIS ARMS WISHING
TO TAKE DAMIEN.

DEL HANDS DAMIEN TO ROD AND
ROD CONTINUES THE DANCE. ROD
BEHAVES IN A VERY
AFFECTIONATE/UNCLE WAY TO
DAMIEN. TICKLING THE KID AND
MAKING HIM LAUGH AS HE DANCES
ROUND THE ROOM.

NOW ROD COMES TO THE MIRROR ON
WALL (FOR THIS SCENE ONLY WE
WILL NEED A MUCH LARGER MIRROR
THEN WE NORMALLY HAVE IN THE
FLAT.)

ROD LOOKS IN MIRROR AND REACTS
MYSTIFIED.

WE NOW SEE FROM RODS POV THAT
DAMIEN IS MISSING FROM THE
REFLECTION - IT IS SIMPLY ROD,
WITH HIS ARM IN THE POSE OF
HOLDING THE CHILD, AND A
DISEMBODIED BALLOON FLOATING
IN THE AIR.

2

AWAY FROM MIRROR, ROD DOUBLE
CHECKS AND WE SEE HE IS STILL
HOLDING DAMIEN.

HE LOOKS BACK AT MIRROR AND
AGAIN DAMIEN IS MISSING.

ROD REACTS TOTALLY HORRIFIED,
OPEN HIS MOUTH TO LET OUT A
CRY.

SHARP CUT TO:

2. INT. ROD & CASSY'S

    BEDROOM. STUDIO. NIGHT.

ROD AND CASSY ARE IN BED. CASSY
IS FAST ASLEEP.

FROM THE DREAM/NIGHTMARE ROD
LETS OUT A CRY OF ALARM, THERE
ARE BEADS OF SWEAT ON HIS
BROW.

HE WAKES FROM THE NIGHTMARE
AND SUCKS IN AIR IN RAPID
BREATHS.

HE CHECKS RADIO/ALARM CLOCK.

IT STANDS AT 5.59 A.M.

RODNEY:
(DEEPLY DEPRESSED) Oh, God!

Not another day!!

ROD LAYS FOR AWHILE, CALMS
HIMSELF AND REGAINS SOME OF
HIS LOST COMPOSURE.

THE RADIO/ALARM CLOCK NOW
SWITCHES TO 6.00 A.M AND
"MERRY CHRISTMAS" BY SLADE
BEGINS PLAYING FROM RADIO-
ALARM.

ROD SWITCHES IT OFF QUICKLY.

4

CASSANDRA:
(WITHOUT OPENING HER
EYES)(MUMBLES) What's the
time?

RODNEY:
It's time for us to emigrate
or at least discuss the
advantages of cryogenics.

CASSANDRA:
And how are we feeling this
morning?

RODNEY:
Great! How else could I feel?
I'm thirty one years of age
and I work for Trotters
Independent Traders.

CASSANDRA:
There are lots of people who'd
give their right arm to be in
your position.

RODNEY:
I know, but they're all tucked
up safe and sound in their
padded-cells.

5

BBC ENTERTAINMENT, COMEDY
REHEARSAL SCRIPT
WITH RE-WRITES 30.9.96

50/LEG M061F

JOHN.S

ONLY FOOLS & HORSES
SERIES 8
BY
JOHN SULLIVAN

EPISODE 1

'HEROES AND VILLAINS'

JOHN. S

S.4 - 13
.6 - 40
7 - 50
8 - 56
9 - 66
19 - 111

****

EXEC PRODUCER	**JOHN SULLIVAN**
PRODUCER	**GARETH GWENLAN**
DIRECTOR	**TONY DOW**
Associate Producer	SUE LONGSTAFF
1st A.D.	DAVID REID
Location Manager	LISA McARTHUR
Production Assistant	CAROLINE GARDENER
2nd A.D. (Props)	BECCY FAWCETT
2nd A.D. (Artists)	DOMINIC BOWLES
Production Secretary	KATIE WILKINSON

****

Overall filming dates	3rd - 26th October 1996
Rehearsal dates	4th - 13th November 1996
Studio	14th & 15th November 1996

****

Production Office	Room 7012 TVC
Telephone	0181 576 9902
Fax	0181 576 9906

SCENE 1/11. INT VAN LOCATION. EXT. (DAY 3). NIGHT. 2230.

DEL:
(ALMOST AS IF IT'S ROD'S FAULT) What are

we gonna do now, eh?

ROD:
I don't know, Derek! We are stuck in the middle

of Peckham at 10.30 at night dressed up as

Batman and Robin! You - you picked these

costumes! I wanted to go as The Blues

Brothers!

DEL:
Rodney, we'd have still broken down and been

stuck in this embarrassing situation!

ROD:
Oh yeah! We'd have both been wearing suits

and ties - what right zooms we'd have looked!

DEL:
But we'd never have won first prize as The

Blues Brothers!

ROD:
At least we could have walked home!

BBC TV Comedy
welcomes you to tonight's recording of

ONLY FOOLS
and
HORSES

Written by
John Sullivan

Produced by
Gareth Gwenlan

Directed by
Tony Dow

DEL:
Stop moaning! We gotta think of a way out of

this.

ROD:
Alright, let's think about it. (PRODUCES

MOBILE PHONE) We can phone the RAC.

DEL:
Yes, ask to be put through to their Broken Down

Whilst Dressed Like A Couple Of Prats

department?

ROD:
What about the police?

DEL:
The police!! We'd never live it down, Rodney.

Our lives would be hell! We'd have to emigrate.

ROD:
At this moment in time that doesn't sound a bad

alternative.

DEL:
Alright, let's think about this situation.

ROD:
Oh, do we have to!!

DEL:
There's always a way, Rodney. Let's sit here and think.

ROD:
Del, the pubs'll be chucking out soon. They'll tear us to shreds.

DEL:
Listen, we are much closer to old Harry's house than we are to home. If we run we could be there in five minutes.

ROD:
But we'll be seen! People on buses. People in restaurant windows!

DEL:
Not if we go through the back streets and the alleys. All you got down there are winos and crackheads and they see Batman and Robin every night.... Come on, we can do it.

ROD:
.... Five minutes?

DEL:
Five minutes if we hurry.

ROD:
Oh jeez!....

SCENE 1/12. BACK STREETS/TOWNHALL. LOCATION. EXT. (DAY 3). NIGHT. 2230.

THIS IS A STREET THAT RUNS ALONG THE BACK OF THE TOWN HALL.

THERE IS A BACK DOOR ABOVE WHICH IS SOME KIND OF COAT-OF-ARMS (OR SOMETHING TO TELL US THIS IS THE TOWN HALL.

PARKED OPPOSITE, AND CLOSE TO THE CORNER OF AN ALLEY OR A SMALL STREET, IS A MODERN CAR (DRIVERS DOOR TO PAVEMENT)

THE BACK DOOR TO TOWN HALL IS OPENED BY A COMMISSIONAIRE AND COUNCILLOR MURRAY EXITS CARRYING HANDBAG AND BRIEFCASE.

COMMISSIONAIRE:
Goodnight Councillor Murray.

MURRAY:
Good night, Tom.

THE DOOR CLOSES AND CLL MURRAY MAKES HER WAY ACROSS ROAD TO CAR.

SHE STOPS AT DRIVERS DOOR AND OPENS HER HANDBAG FOR CAR KEYS.

AT THIS POINT DAWN (THE GIRL MEMBER OF MUGGING GANG) RUSHES ROUND CORNER APPARENTLY IN A WILD PANIC.

DAWN:
Sorry, Miss, have you seen a policeman round

here?

MURRAY:
No, I haven't!

    IMMEDIATELY GARY (THE LEADER)
    STEP OUT FROM BEHIND CORNER.

GARY:
Good! Giss your money!!

MURRAY:
What are you doing? (CALLS) Tom!

    THE OTHER MEMBERS OF GANG,
    SCOTT AND KEVIN HAVE NOW
    APPEARED AND THE MUGGING
    BEGINS.

    WE'LL NEED AD-LIBS FOR MOST OF
    IT.

GARY:
Get her handbag!!

MURRAY:
Help!!

SCOTT:
Someone shut her up!

    DAWN PUTS HER HAND ROUND
    MURRAY'S MOUTH.

KEVIN:
She's got a diamond ring on her finger.

    SCOTT NOW SEES SOMETHING UP
    THE ROAD THAT MAKES HIM FREEZE
    IN INCREDULITY. HE NUDGES GARY.

SCOTT:
Gary! (GESTURES UP ROAD)

GARY LOOKS AND FREEZES.

DAWN AND KEVIN AND NOW MURRAY
ALL DO LIKEWISE.

WE SEE FROM THEIR POV:

TWO HUNDRED YARDS AWAY
BATMAN AND ROBIN ARE RUNNING
TOWARDS THEM.

SOUND OVER: BATMAN THEME.

GARY:
(INCREDULOUSLY) What's happening?

MURRAY:
(EQUALLY INCREDULOUSLY) I haven't the

faintest idea!

GARY:
(TERRIFIED)(TO REST OF GANG) Go!!

THE GANG RUN OFF LEAVING
MURRAY OPEN-MOUTHED IN
DISBELIEF.

BATMAN AND ROBIN NOW RUN PAST
HER.

(SUGGEST SHE DOES DOUBLE HEAD
TURN - ONE FOR BATMAN, ONE FOR
ROBIN)

BATMAN NOW STOPS - ROBIN STOPS
A BIT FURTHER ON.

DEL:
It's Councillor Murray, isn't it?

Page: 86 of 115

MURRAY:
(FRIGHTENED) Yes.

DEL:
I recognise you from your photograph. Derek

Trotter. You may remember I wrote to you some

time ago about a gr....

ROD:
Del, let's go!

DEL:
Yes. Well, must dash. Maybe another time?

BATMAN AND ROBIN RUSH OFF.

MURRAY WATCHES THEM STILL IN
TOTAL SHOCK.

BBC ENTERTAINMENT

6A. 2nd DRAFT @ 28/02/02 (44)

JOHN S

WRITTEN BY JOHN SULLIVAN

EPISODE THREE
'SLEEPLESS IN PECKHAM'

Executive Producer ....JOHN SULLIVAN
Producer...GARETH GWENLAN
Director...TONY DOW

D H

THE SENDING OF THIS SCRIPT DOES NOT CONSTITUTE AN OFFER OF A CONTRACT OR A PART
THEREIN

37: EXT. THE CEMETERY/GRAVESIDE. DAY.

ONE WEEK LATER.

FROM A DISTANCE THE MONUMENT IS BRIGHT AND CLEAN.

WE FIND A VAN PARKED CLOSE-BY WHICH BEARS SIGNS REVEALING IT IS THAT OF A STONE-MASON.

ROD, DRESSED SMARTLY, BUT WEARING ONE MARIGOLD GLOVE, PAYS THE MAN SOME MONEY AND THE VAN WILL DRIVE OFF.

WE SEE A PRAM (ONE OF THOSE CARRY-COTS ON WHEELS.

ROD LOOKS INTO PRAM. WE SEE THE LATEST BABY TROTTERESS LYING ASLEEP IN PRAM.

TO ONE SIDE THERE IS THE SECOND MARIGOLD GLOVE, SOME KITCHEN TONGS AND A BLACK BIN LINER IN WHICH, WE ASSUME, LIES THE HYPODERMIC SYRINGES, BEER CANS, ETC. WHICH THIS TIME ROD HAS CLEARED UP.

ROD SITS ON BENCH AND JUST STARES AT MONUMENT. HE IS FILLED WITH A MIX OF EMOTIONS - THE ONLY TEARS HE CRIES ARE IN THE SOUL.

105

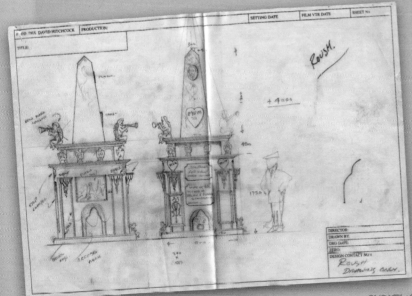

ROD:
(BEAT. BEAT. BEAT. (QUIETLY TO MUM) Did you love him?
....
Did he love you?...........
I hope he made you happy....You know, a few laughs........
I've got two photos of you. And you think... That's it. That's your past Rodney. There's your history... Two photos... And one of 'em's blurred...... (HE LOOKS AT HIS CHILD) I hope she'll be as lovely as you......... She will...... I wish I'd known you....... I wish we'd had.... you know.... something to..... just something.

WE NOW HEAR THE POP, POP SOUND OF THE THREE WHEEL VAN APPROACHING AND WE SEE DEL ARRIVE IN BACKGROUND.

ROD:
(TO MONUMENT) If you bump into Uncle Albert, say thanks.

DEL ALIGHTS FROM VAN AND APPROACHES ROD.

DEL:
Alright, Rodders. Bin looking for you.

ROD:
I just thought I'd take her for a walk.... Did a bit of cleaning up.

DEL:
Yeah, good boy. (LOOKS INTO PRAM) Heartbreaker, ain she?..... She got a name yet?

106

ROD:
Mmmh....

ROD GESTURES TO MONUMENT.

WE SEE THE MONUMENT NOW READS:

JOAN MAVIS TROTTER

FELL ASLEEP MARCH 12TH 1964

WIFE OF REG

MOTHER OF DEL-BOY AND RODNEY

GRANDMOTHER OF DAMIEN AND (THE FRESHLY CARVED NAME OF ROD AND CASSIES CHILD)

DEL SEES THE BABY'S NAME.

DEL SMILES AND CLOSES HIS EYES TIGHT WITH EMOTION.

DEL NUDGES RODNEY AND SMILES HIS GRATITUDE.

ROD NUDGES HIM BACK AND RETURNS THE SMILE.

ROD:
Getting a bit cold for little 'un.

DEL:
Yeah.... Come on, I'll stick the pram in the boot.

THEY BEGIN REMOVING THE CARRYCOT AND FOLDING PRAM DOWN, ETC.

NOW THE ONE THING DEL DIDN'T WANT TO HAPPEN, HAPPENS.

ROD:
Del, can I ask you a question?

107

DEL CLOSES HIS EYES IN DREAD - HE
KNOWS WHAT'S COMING.

DEL:
Wha'sat?

ROD:
Other than looks, was he like me
in any way?

DEL:
Who?

ROD:
You know who! Freddie Robdal. My
father.

DEL:
...... Freddie the Frog was a
professional burglar. He was
disloyal to his friends, he was a
womaniser, a home-breaker, a
conman, a thief, a liar and a
cheat........ So, no, Rodney,
you're nothing like him.

ROD SMILES - DEL'S WORD MEANT A
LOT TO HIM.

DEL:
Let's go home... bruv.

CUT TO:

38:   EXT. LONDON ROADS. DAY.

WE SEE THE THREE WHEEL VAN
DRIVING AWAY FROM US (WE DO NOT
ACTUALLY SEE DEL AND ROD, SO WE
HAVE NO IDEA WHERE THE BABY IS:
WHICH GETS US OVER ALL THE SAFETY
ISSUES AND ANORAKISH LETTERS.)

WE HEAR DEL AND ROD OVER:

THE END   108

ACKNOWLEDGEMENTS

First and foremost, thanks must go to John Sullivan for creating such wonderful characters that have given us all so much fun over the years. Similarly, all of the incredibly talented cast and crew who helped to bring the characters to life deserve a huge 'thank you.'

For their help in pulling this book together, thanks go to David Hitchcock, James Conway, Heather Jones, Michelle Dewar and Lynn and Ben Kirby as well as Only Fools afficianado Perry Aghajanoff, whose amazing collection of memorabilia and merchandise is an absolute treasure trove.

For their patience and perseverance, thanks to Lorna Russell and Charlotte Macdonald. Also, for his creative input and design talent, thank you, Mike Jones.

Finally, Jim Sullivan has been a fantastic help, contributing ideas and checking details to keep the characters true to themselves and to the series.

LOVELY JUBBLY!

This time next year...
we could be billionaires!